∞

Our Journey to God

Fr. Maurice Nkem Emelu

Our Journey to God

∞

Exploring the Power of Faith
from Abraham to You

EWTN PUBLISHING, INC.
Irondale, Alabama

Nihil obstat: Monsignor Stephen Frost, *Censor Librorum*

Imprimatur: Most Reverend Armando X. Ochoa, D.D.
Bishop of Fresno, February 17, 2017

EWTN Publishing, Inc.
5817 Old Leeds Road, Irondale, AL 35210

Distributed by Sophia Institute Press, Box 5284, Manchester, NH 03108.

Library of Congress Cataloging-in-Publication Data

Names: Emelu, Maurice Nkem, author.
Title: Our journey to God : exploring the power of faith from Abraham to you
/ Fr. Maurice Nkem Emelu.
Description: Irondale, Alabama : EWTN Publishing, Inc., 2017.
Identifiers: LCCN 2017006479 | ISBN 9781682780404 (pbk. : alk. paper)
Subjects: LCSH: Faith—Biblical teaching. | Catholic Church—Doctrines.
Classification: LCC BS680.F27 E46 2017 | DDC 234/.23 —dc23 LC record
available at https://lccn.loc.gov/2017006479

First printing

*To atheists, skeptics, and agnostics, in their daily
search for meaning—for the grace of faith*

*To those dealing with some forms of doubt in their
faith journey—for the grace of divine enlightenment*

To believers—for the grace of fidelity

Contents

∞

Foreword

Fr. Emelu's insightful exploration of the journey of faith employs a deep and delightful method, weaving together theoretical explanations, biblical and African stories, and genuine solutions to stubborn practical problems. He begins with an overview of four stages of faith—from wonder to rational reflection to relationship to lived Christianity—and then he plunges into the mysterious and adventurous depths of the last two stages through his dialectic of ironic stories and rational reflection.

For Fr. Emelu, faith is a journey with a supremely loving and provident personal God—filled with invitation, surprise, adventure, self-sacrifice, doubts, enlightened resolutions, growth, loving service, and, in the end, redemption and salvation. There is no simple explanation of it, because as his many diverse stories show, the journey is different for everyone. Yet if we trust in the One who makes Himself known to us, remain faithful to Him even in times of great challenge and doubt, give thanks for hidden graces, and follow His lead in service and surrender, we will never be disappointed. Rather, we will be the recipients of an inexpressible love and joy—not only in the next life, but in glimpses and sparks along faith's way. I recommend this book not only to those seeking deeper faith, but also to those who are curious but as yet uncommitted.

—Fr. Robert J. Spitzer, S.J., Ph.D.
President, Magis Center of Reason and Faith

∞

Acknowledgments

Many people contributed to making this book a reality.

Bishop Augustine Ukwuoma of the Catholic Diocese of Orlu, Nigeria, my local ordinary, inspired the initial interest for this work and graciously endorsed it. I am very grateful to him.

My appreciation goes out to Cornelius Fontem Esua, Archbishop of Bamenda, Cameroon, who read the manuscript and gave a wonderful endorsement as well.

Bishop Armando Ochoa, in whose Diocese of Fresno I have resided for the past five years, created the pastoral environment that enabled me to develop this book in the way I had envisioned it — growth in love and knowledge of the Faith. I am exceedingly grateful to him for endorsing the book and granting the imprimatur.

I am equally grateful to Msgr. Stephen Frost, pastor of Christ the King Church in Bakersfield, California, who read the manuscript in a brief period and granted the nihil obstat.

Similarly, I am grateful to Fr. Robert Spitzer, president of the Magis Center. Despite his tight schedule, he made time to write the thought-provoking foreword, as well as endorse the book.

My gratitude goes to Dr. Tina Facca-Meiss, Associate Professor of Marketing and Director of the Program in Non-Profit Administration at John Carroll University. She read the manuscript and gave a beautiful endorsement as well.

I am grateful to Charles McKinney, president of Sophia Institute Press; Michael Warsaw, president of EWTN Publications Inc.; Brandon McGinley and the rest of the editorial team at both publishing houses for their editorial efficiency and publication in record time.

Kathy Andes did the first copy edit of the raw manuscript before it went to the publisher. I am thankful for her work in crossing the t's and dotting the i's, alongside my adopted mom, Jeanne Curran, and my administrative secretary, Mary Ann Verderber, who both offered helpful feedback.

The board and executives of my Gratia Vobis Ministries were a source of inspiration to me during the development of this work. Their support is greatly appreciated.

My dad, Alphaeus Emelu, and my late mom, Grace, through whom I first received the gift of faith, deserve my enduring gratitude. They sowed the seed, and God provided the grace.

Finally, I am eternally indebted to God, from whose wisdom I have received both the skill and the gift to write. To Him be the glory. Amen.

∞

Our Journey to God

∞

Introduction

At the time, it seemed like a gathering gleaned from the margins of society. Yet what happened in Jerusalem's Upper Room more than two thousand years ago shaped the thoughts and lives of so many like no other event in human history. The succinct description of the event in the Acts of the Apostles shows its groundbreaking impact. Out of the Upper Room (also called the Cenacle on Mount Zion), the once timid band of apostles and disciples, numbering about 120, spread the Good News to the ends of the world. These were men — and a few women — who had little education. And by Jewish standards, they had no credentials to catapult them to popularity and leadership. They were simply ordinary men and women of Galilee.

No sooner had they stepped out of that room in Jerusalem than their works and voices echoed to the ends of the earth. Inspired by an inner motivation, they broke the boundaries of fear and pride, allowing themselves to be moved by the life-changing encounter of the New Pentecost. Generation after generation celebrates their lives as the pioneers of Christianity and Western culture. How did they do it?

It all began with simple faith. The Lord Jesus Christ had asked them to stay in Jerusalem until the fulfillment of the promise of the Father. They may not have fully understood what "stay in Jerusalem" meant or would bring, but they waited anyway. Hoping against all hope, trusting against all trust, believing against all conventional beliefs, and struggling with the worst fears, they kept a novena of surrender to the rule of faith. Theirs was a beautiful example of the obedience of faith and faith in action. It paid off, as it always does.

History is replete with similar stories — men and women who did the humanly impossible by faith. From the biblical and historical accounts of the lives of Abraham and Moses, to the lives of the prophets, the apostles, the early Fathers of the Church, and every individual who has been fired by an encounter with divinity, there is one commonality: They all have faith in God lived out in their daily lives. To explore this connecting thread uniting all these men and women is the goal of this book.

Using biblical figures as case studies and interspersed with personal experiences through the prism of African and Western worldviews — some born out of many years of pastoral ministry — this book looks at how the journey of faith evolves. It examines the nature of faith as well as those essential elements capable of transforming lives and society. These elements can revolutionize the way you look at the Christian faith. They may also enable you to see anew things you might have taken for granted about human destiny, moving you to ask the most fundamental questions about life — yours and others'.

The first five chapters will explore the nature of faith. Drawing from numerous experiences, we will discuss the characteristics of faith as lived in the lives of Moses; Abraham; Mary, the Mother of the Lord; and many other figures. We will pay special

Introduction

attention to the obstacles to faith and the tools for overcoming those obstacles as we unveil the paradoxes of the faith journey. The relationship between faith, hope, and charity will be discussed as well.

In the last six chapters, we will explore the content of faith, zeroing in on a few attributes distinguishing true objects of faith from false ones, so as to see the benefits of true faith. Although orthodox Catholic theology will form the basis of these reflections, the application will reflect some of the commonalities among all Christian believers—showing that faith, as our common heritage, should unite us.

Faith is not an individual's private dominion. It is the core of our identity as religious beings. It is the substance of things we hope for. My hope for you is that these words will lead you to a greater appreciation of the transforming power of faith.

Part 1

The Nature of Faith

Chapter 1

∞

A Life-Changing Ride

An author's literary style is shaped by the culture in which he grew up, learned, and lived. This is as true of William Shakespeare as it is of G. K. Chesterton and his friend C. S. Lewis. As an African, I grew up in a culture where the best of ideas are developed through narrative — collections of stories. From folktales to proverbs, much of African heritage is a nursery full of comic allusions. Stories are like spices garnishing the rich main courses on the table of ideas. It will, therefore, be consistent with my background to introduce this chapter (and spice up other chapters) with a funny African story.

A certain man from a village in a West African country rode his new bicycle to a nearby market square to shop for his groceries. After an incredible shopping trip — many of the items on his list were on sale — he was so excited that he forgot he came to the market on his new bicycle. And so he went home, leaving his bicycle behind. In the morning, when he was leaving for work, he went to the spot where he usually parked his bicycle and discovered that it wasn't there, and it occurred to him that he forgot the bicycle at the market square. Aware of the notoriety of the market square as a beehive for thieves, the man concluded that his bicycle would likely have been stolen. Worried, he resorted to prayer, asking God to please keep his bicycle safe until he arrived at the square.

When he reached the market square, he was very happy to find his bicycle safely parked where he left it. He believed, and rightly so, that his prayers were answered. Overjoyed as someone who has just won a lottery, he jumped onto his bicycle, singing and praising God as he rode home. On his way, he sighted a village chapel close by and decided to go in and thank God for answering his prayers. He stayed for about five minutes. No sooner had he come out of the chapel than he saw that his bicycle had been stolen! Disappointed and frustrated, he went back into the chapel, looked up, and said, "God, is this real? You've got to be kidding me!"

This light story illustrates the paradox of life and of faith — a paradox that will be explored in greater depth in a later chapter on faith and doubt. But first let's have a primer on the basics of faith: What is faith? And when does the journey of faith begin?

Faith is a form of knowledge of God. And for us humans, the journey of faith, like the learning of any knowledge, ordinarily proceeds from the simple to the complex, from the known to the unknown. This process makes sense especially because the concept of "faith" in the Christian sense includes connotations of transcendence and profundity in addition to the simply not-yet-fully-known. It is the movement from the known to the unknown, from the here and now to the transcendent, from the superficial to the profound, that makes a faith journey a comedy of a sort; the key players are those who are limited by time and space, and the One who is beyond time and space. The comedy has the qualities of suspense, expectation, irony, plot, and resolution — a resolution that, on God's terms, always ends in joy and happiness.

A Life-Changing Ride

Growing up in the eastern part of Nigeria, I had often been fascinated by the beauties of the physical sphere—the orderliness of nature, the complexities and marvels of the world. I recall one moment in particular that blew my mind. It occurred when my dad took me to the western coastal city of Lagos to see Bar Beach on the Atlantic Ocean. It was the first time I saw the ocean, and it was a breathtaking sight!

I watched the waves and saw how the waters seemed to merge with the sky on the horizon. The spectacle kept me thinking and asking questions in order to understand the complexities and orderliness of this beautiful world. Some of my questions were answered by my parents, some by my teachers, relatives, or friends, and others by the pastor of my church. In addition, in quiet, private moments, I came to some conclusions about existence beyond what my external senses could see or perceive. I couldn't repress this nascent curiosity without doing harm to what is natural to me as a human being.

Although my suppositions may not have been totally coherent, they flowed naturally from my inner being just as we all thirst for water or hunger for food. I was a child thirsting for something, something beyond what my physical senses could fathom. In sum, I was reacting to an inherent impetus to know the source of goodness, beauty, and truth. Fascinating nature was, for me, an indicator of some greater truth and then a revelation of that truth. It created the stage for this dramatic journey in which I was a curious actor as well as a spectator, trying to solve the fantastic riddles set before me. I didn't set it up. I was simply brought into it.

My experience is similar to many others', and maybe yours. Have you ever had to make sense of evidence around you and put the puzzle of life together? Have you pondered why there are things instead of nothing, why the physical world is the way it is, and why the force of gravity and other laws of the physical world are the way they are? Do you sometimes wonder and inquire: What is the origin of your life and the lives of your parents and grandparents all the way back to the first man and woman who ever lived? What is your destiny? How have living things come to be? Have you ever asked who is responsible for the perfections that we see in the world, or for the genesis of time itself?

These basic questions express a deep-seated sense of wonder that is natural to us as humans. They are at first methodologically scientific because all science begins with the desire to know and a sense of wonder; but, above all, they are also philosophical and theological because they emanate from our rationality and allude to our innate religious nature. When you ask these or similar questions, you are asking about the fundamental *why* and *who* of existence and not just the rudimentary *how* of empirical explanations; and you have started a journey that will change your life forever. You have started a *faith* journey.

This is, I contend, the first stage of the faith journey. If you will, you have been admitted into the nursery school of faith. Welcome! The school of faith is a journey with one exceptional end goal — the Beatific Vision. Its culmination is a graduation feast, second to none you have ever known, or could ever imagine. "What no eye has seen, nor ear heard, nor the heart of man conceived, [is] what God has prepared for those who love him" (1 Cor. 2:9).

Let us classify faith in four main stages:

- A sense of appreciation and wonder for our environment — the beautiful and complex physical world and creatures
- Knowledge of God through the natural light of human reason

- Knowledge of God through revelation and by faith
- The life of faith—a personal response to God in a relationship

These stages are the steps by which faith evolves from the known to the unknown, from the elementary forms of divine realization to the deeper awareness of His being, culminating in a personal relationship with God. The stages flow into and interact with one another, for they are not always discrete; instead, they are integrated. In this chapter, however, we will discuss them in logical sequence—no chronological ordering is intended. We cannot totally encompass faith in a linear logical progression because the object of faith is God, and He exceeds all our human interpretations. Not to mention that humans are complex and dynamic; individuals encounter God in different ways, and their explanations of the encounter differ from person to person.

But, as I hope you will see, these four stages demonstrate a recognizable process by which we can come to know God. Join me as we embark on this faith ride!

Appreciation and Wonder

The first stage of the faith journey could be described as a mixed sense of appreciation and wonder of our environment—the beautiful and complex physical world, including living creatures. God makes Himself known through the beauty of the physical world. We come to realize this imprint of divinity by the gift of rationality He has given us. And so the sense of wonder and curiosity that initiates any search for knowledge is simply part of the natural disposition to seek God.

Many great men and women of faith started or enriched their faith journey this way. St. Francis of Assisi was renowned for his deep connection with nature and his ability to see the imprint of divinity communicated through nature. He found God's fingerprint in nature, and he deepened his relationship with God through contemplation of His beautiful handiwork. The Little Flower, St. Thérèse of Lisieux, had a special connection with nature, so much so that she could see the profundity of God in every flower. Flowers, canyons, flowing waters, seasons — nature's serenity reveals its order, and its order implies an Orderer.

This curiosity might also begin with looking at ourselves — at human beings, the apex of creation, whose beauties and complexities make us wonder how we have been so intricately made. The psalmist draws from this aspect of God's creatures in lyrics about the heavens and natural law — the orderliness of divine law flowing from the orderliness of natural law, which in turn flows from the perfection of the Creator: "The heavens are telling the glory of God; and the firmament proclaims his handiwork" (Ps. 19:1).

There have also been rich theological and philosophical discussions, especially during the medieval period, based on evidence from the natural world testifying to God's revelation. For the most part, these discussions were in response to critics, skeptics, and atheists for whom faith was a farce or, at best, a kindly illusion. (We can see this play out, for instance, in the proofs of God's existence offered by Sts. Augustine, Anselm, and Thomas Aquinas.) We are seeing a resurgence of interest in the revelatory aspect of nature in our postmodern world as both secular and religious thinkers look at nature with new eyes. The bottom line is that nature has a language: It speaks the language of its Maker and draws us into contemplation.

Thus, this stage of the knowledge of God consistently enriches our understanding of divinity because our knowledge of

Him is corroborated and enhanced by our experiences of the physical world. Or, put in another way, it is both natural and rational to see God revealed through nature. I cannot emphasize it enough: The physical world is revelatory.

Nonetheless, there is a great danger if the knowledge of God is limited to an appreciation of nature. If nature becomes the origin *and* end of our contemplation, we fall into serious error. Many people and cultures through history have stopped their search for God at observation of nature, resulting in nature cults and pantheism, in which "God" becomes a being or an element who is *part of* the material world. The center of the worship becomes *nature itself* and not the Maker of nature. This is a disastrous aberration from true worship. This error can also lead to polytheism — the belief in many gods. This is a recipe for superstition, a caricature of the true creedal journey.

A concrete example from African Traditional Religion, which is regarded as a nature religion, may help clarify this point. Odomankoma is a deity of the Ashanti people of Ghana in West Africa. Before the arrival of Christianity, Odomankoma was viewed by its followers (notice we use *its* rather than *his* or *her*) as the origin of order in the universe, and some also saw it as the source of the universe. The Ashanti were inspired by the awe-inspiring orderliness of the universe; they translated this wonder into a search for the transcendent. Additionally, face-to-face with the reality and fear of death and pestilence, they sought answers to life and its origin. And so they figured out that there was definitely a higher being beyond the physical world, whom they identified as Odomankoma.

As far as it goes, they were correct: There is a Being who transcends all aspects of our ordinary lives, and what we call Him doesn't particularly matter. (Arabic-speaking Christians, for instance, call God "Allah.") Their religious practice, however, shows how they lost the way on their journey of contemplation of the divine. When the native Ashanti identified this "being," they began to garb it with human qualities; they had created a nature god. They had gone so far toward the ultimate transcendence of the real God, but not far enough. This instance suggests how limited the *unaided* human mind is in the knowledge it can discern about God.

Greek mythology, with its pantheon of gods, expresses in a different way the same credulity in nature gods. There are stories that show how the gods marry and give in to lust, violence, and other common human vices compatible with a purely materialistic existence. At this basic level of contemplation, people's conception of their god or gods remains self-referential; they can only imagine a god who is like us, but more powerful. They have made a discovery, namely, the awareness of the existence of the supernatural. Nonetheless, their articulation of this discovery in religious cult is anthropomorphic. Thus, their worship is idolatrous since their gods are simply human creations filling the void of the supernatural. Scripture speaks of such gods with severe disapproval:

> Their idols are silver and gold, the work of men's hands.
> They have mouths, but do not speak; eyes, but do not see.
> They have ears, but do not hear; noses, but do not smell.
> They have hands, but do not feel; feet, but do not walk;
> and they do not make a sound in their throat. Those who
> make them are like them; so are all who trust in them.
> (Ps. 115:4–8)

Thus, we can abstract the reality of the Creator from the physical world, but we may not conceive His nature as a being entirely set apart from us, holy and supreme over the works of *His* hands. A higher, deeper encounter saves us from this distortion.

Rational Engagement

Knowledge of God gained through the appreciation of the physical world is similar to that gained through the natural light of human reason. Judeo-Christian tradition expresses this level of faith by a convincing and incisive thesis: We are created in the image and likeness of God. We have the faculties, the conscience, the openness to truth, the appreciation of beauty, the desire for happiness, the sense of moral goodness, and the longing for freedom that all tend toward the truth that there is a God and that we have the ability to enter into relationship with Him. Many theologians agree that this knowledge of God is *certain* since it flows from the very nature of the human person, who is a "being for transcendence"—a religious being.

Human reason gives us the necessary tools to engage with the God question. It leads us to make sense of the world and to investigate the whys of things. In spite of the claims of strictly materialistic evolution, reason pierces through the limitations of the physical sphere into the mysteries of life and human destiny. Reason is God's gift for making sense of the depth of the spiritual. Through it, He speaks to us in a silent but powerful way, leading us to ask the most important questions and to find the answers to life and living. Many authorities throughout history have affirmed this truth; Pope St. John Paul II, for instance, in his encyclical *Fides et Ratio* showed clearly the intrinsic connection between faith and reason.

And yet faith cannot be *just* a product of human reason. As Pope Pius XII rightly remarked, many obstacles prevent reason from fulfilling its purpose of knowing and understanding truth.[1] There are limits to what we can know by ourselves, just as there are limits to every human logical construct. Human logic alone, even with the finest of brains, can do little in comparison with the immensity of the divine embrace and divine revelation. St. Thomas Aquinas is a good example: After composing his renowned volumes about God and theology, he saw a glimpse of divine glory and confessed that all he had written about God was like straw.

Similarly, the limitations of unaided reason are such that we do not always know that we do not know something! A person with a genuine thirst for the truth will acknowledge this limitation and be willing to search for help to overcome these limitations. This first requires some outside guidance to identify the ignorance to which we are blinded. We move first to knowledge that we did previously know; then we proceed to understanding and certainty. An illustration may help clarify this idea.

A member of a remote tribe in the rain forest might not know or even have speculated that man has invented the airplane and therefore can fly. He has never seen an airplane and has only observed and believed that heavy objects always fall to the earth. He never knew something could exist that is heavier than air that would not fall to the earth immediately.

In this case, his reason alone would not only be unable to discover the fact of the existence of airplanes, but it might lead him to the wrong conclusion based on his limited experience. Similarly, divine revelation tells us about things that our minds

---

[1] Pius XII, Encyclical *Humani generis* ("Concerning Some False Opinions Threatening to Undermine the Foundations of Catholic Doctrine"), August 12, 1950, no. 2.

didn't even know we didn't know were true — things we couldn't have imagined. In our example, an outsider could explain to the tribesman that airplanes exist and do fly. At this point, after the "revelation" from the outsider, the tribesman's journey to truth has advanced to where he knows that he doesn't understand much about airplanes — but he now knows that they exist.

Reason alone, unaided by God, has its limitations. It certainly cannot lead us to an intimate relationship with Him. But it can lead us to the elementary knowledge that is available to any person by virtue of having been made in God's image and likeness. It may also lead us to moral principles that are in line with the good, which flows from the natural law. And the natural law is consistent with reason.

But the opposite is not always the case; that is, although natural law is discoverable by reason, that does not mean that reason always gets it right because human reason, when not properly formed, can make judgments that are rebellious to its own purpose — that is, the truth — and opposed to the laws of nature. Thus, its judgment could sometimes be defective, resulting in decisions and practices that oppose true faith and are against the natural law and sound moral norms. Examples of such practices include witchcraft, voodoo practices, black magic, sorcery, and ritual murder as practiced by some traditional religions or, more recently, terrorism built on the erroneous relationship between faith and reason present in Islam, where these two concepts are sometimes placed at odds with one another.

On the other hand, the defective judgment of reason could also lead to a deep doubt that discourages us from engaging with the supernatural, preferring instead to focus on the experiential, worldly realm of human reasoning. Thus, reason limits itself, well, unreasonably. This undermines the very nature of rationality, which learns from the experiential but also ought to transcend it.

This is where atheism enters the picture. Atheism is an escape in response to that which is beyond human imagining — the supernatural. Defective reasoning has an alibi; it simply denies what it cannot fathom on its own. Atheism is the ultimate fruit of this denial, with skepticism and agnosticism as its milder forms.

Could this not properly be explained in terms of a fear of engaging with the supernatural? You might think that with the advancement of knowledge, science, and technology in our time — so-called human progress — we might also be better able to pierce through human limitations regarding understanding the supernatural. But just the opposite has taken place: We have retreated from the supernatural and limited our rationality to making sense only of things that can be proven in the laboratory. This neuters the thrill of the epic in our sojourn in life — and our discovery of the true and ultimate meaning of life. Unfortunately, many are hesitant or unwilling to engage in the all-important inquiry into the deepest aspects of human life and spirituality. Instead, they consider the *why* of things and life as mere abstractions, tossing aside the very core of our rational nature. This is escapism; may I even call it cowardly? Audacity in engaging reality beyond the experimental demonstrates strength and opens us to incredible beauty.

So, defective reason can lead to doubt and even to despair of the reality of the supernatural. Another problem with remaining at the rational level of the appreciation of God, though, is the chance of fashioning a rationalistic god. Such was the temptation of rationalists such as René Descartes, Immanuel Kant, and the modern positivistic ideologists and even the new-age propagandists who want God to be understood in terms only of what the human mind can logically approve or demonstrate; or some astral energy explained in terms of matter and a form of a god within, that is, a domesticated god (and also a bizarre attempt to make the divine rationally accessible by just, well, making things up); or a being realized through the finest progress—evolution—of the human mind. This last theory describes a god that would eventually need to be improved upon as history evolves, since this god's identity is shaped by and through history, and when this deity has maxed out its relevance, it ceases to be. It "progresses" to extinction, when the human person no longer needs the cloak of divinity; we will have, some insist on believing, divinized ourselves by our own progress.

Hence, if the danger of limiting our knowledge of God to the appreciation of nature is superstition, then the danger of using unaided human reason to access the deepest of divine mysteries is making a god of the mind—a rationalistic god. One common feature in both cases is that the traditional concept of God is viewed as either threatening or irrelevant. In both of these cases, He must be rejected, denied, or ignored so that man can be the ruler of himself.

Both of these errors totally exclude the possibility of a God-human relationship. Thus, it is dangerous not to pass the level of a nature-based, rationalistic appreciation of divinity to the next stage of the faith journey. The third stage of the journey opens the doors for a richer experience and relationship with God. It is connected with the sense of *wonder* as well as rationality. It builds on both, enriches them both, and surpasses them both. Any worthy search for or encounter with the supernatural should be open to this next level of divine unveiling. It is a form of knowledge of God through revelation and by faith.

Our Journey to God

An Incredible Relationship

In this stage of the journey God becomes known through revelation and by faith. While the appreciation of the physical world and our rational appreciation for the good, the beautiful, and the true put us on the path of divine encounter — they bring us to the door of the divine, and perhaps into the foyer — revelation ushers us into a deeper form of encounter that can develop into a true relationship. But we must remember that the faith journey always begins with God Himself; the relationship depends on our *response*.

Observe the radical distinction between this level of the faith journey and the previous two, in which it seemed, at least from the human point of view, that it was man who searched for God. Here it's God who searches for us, as the poet Francis Thompson depicted in his epic poem *The Hound of Heaven*. Hence, the Church's teaching that faith is a *theological virtue* is perennially relevant. A theological virtue is one that is "infused by God into the souls of the faithful to make them capable of acting as God's children and of meriting eternal life."[2] The classical definition of *faith* in Scripture, used also in the *Catechism of the Catholic Church*, is rendered in the letter to the Hebrews:

> Now faith is the assurance of things hoped for, the conviction of things not seen. For by it the men of old received divine approval. By faith we understand that the world

---

[2] *Catechism of the Catholic Church* (CCC), no. 1813. As the *Catechism* in the context of the teaching on virtues defines it, "Faith is the theological virtue by which we believe in God and believe all that he has said and revealed to us, and that Holy Church proposes for our belief, because he is truth itself" (no. 1814).

was created by the word of God, so that what is seen was made out of things which do not appear. (Heb. 11:1–3)

In the previous levels of the faith journey, it appears that we take the initiative. But at this level, it becomes evident that the whole process, even from the start, has been God's initiative. In essence, we do not choose God; He chooses us. Herein lies the profound beauty and uniqueness of the Christian faith—a faith in which God reveals Himself to us in Christ and welcomes us into an incredible relationship. The Lord Jesus said, "You did not choose me, but I chose you and appointed you that you should go and bear fruit and that your fruit should abide; so that whatever you ask the Father in my name, he may give it to you" (John 15:16).

Christian faith, therefore, is the knowledge of God from the top down, from the oracle of divine wisdom as revealed in space and time. God condescends to meet us because He knows that we cannot reach Him by our natural faculties alone. God knows that the temporal, contingent, limited being cannot adequately comprehend the Eternal Being.

Pope Benedict XVI describes how this revelation is all divine initiative:

> To be sure, the mystery of God forever remains beyond the capacity of our concepts and our reason, our rites and our prayers. And yet, by his revelation God himself communicates with us, he tells us about himself and he makes himself accessible. And we are enabled to listen to his Word and to receive his truth. This, then, is the wonder of faith: God, in his love, creates in us—through the working of the Holy Spirit—the proper conditions for us to recognize his Word. God himself, in his will to

reveal himself to us, to enter into contact with us and to make himself present in history, enables us to listen to him and to receive him.[3]

Through history, God has uniquely revealed Himself. Through the Judeo-Christian tradition, we receive a compelling narrative of this divine unveiling—first, in creation and ancient rites and traditions; and second, by a special choice through Abraham and passed down to his descendants, the children born by faith in God, the Creator and the Liberator. In a more unique way in the fullness of time, God became man, enabling us to have the fullness of God's revelation. Ever since, God's revelatory self has continued to be witnessed through His Body, the Church, in liturgical rites and through the people—especially in their reading and living of God's Word. God's Word revealed to us—the Christ—continues to draw us into an appreciation of the Triune God. This knowledge of God is guaranteed by faith in God, who is the Creator, the Redeemer, and the Sanctifier. Faith therefore becomes our assurance of the revelation of God. As the Angelic Doctor (St. Thomas Aquinas) surmised, "For the faith of which we are speaking does not assent to anything, except because it is revealed by God."[4]

Our authority for faith in the God of revelation is not simply earthly data or natural human reason—although these point to His existence. It is also not even the best academic analysis of religion or theology—although these do bring to light some evidence, it can never be the decisive evidence. The revelation from God Himself is the one and only direct evidence that is eternally

---

[3] Benedict XVI, General Audience, October 18, 2012.
[4] Thomas Aquinas, *Summa theologica*, II-II, Q. 1, art. 1.

unchanging. This form of evidence, which is called *theophany*, is the crux of the faith journey. This is where the certitude of faith is totally distinct from the certitude of secular studies.

We tend to trust experts in their field of knowledge. For instance, when we see a doctor, we trust we will be diagnosed correctly and that our disease will be properly treated. Does the doctor, in whom we trust for our medical health, create his art from nothing? Not at all! The doctor only discovers what has been present in the very cells and genes of the human person and follows the unique laws — the natural laws — of human biology to provide a cure or to render palliative care. So it is with other professional fields in which we believe that expertise guarantees accurate information and guidance.

In a deeper, more profound sense, then, the certitude of faith is based on the infinitely greater and more perfect authority of God, who has revealed Himself through signatures of His power in creatures and through history. *God's presence is discovered, not created, by humans.* Our primary motive for faith in God is not simply the abstract truth of the proposition "God exists," but rather the concrete authority of His revelation of Himself in concert with the indelible divine imprint in every being and throughout existence. Humanity's religious sense is innate. We are all God seekers by our very nature. And we are blessed that God allows us to seek Him.

Let us return to the form of evidence, *theophany*, which I said is the crux of the faith journey. Let's try to sketch out this idea by reference to the story of Moses. His theophany was a divine encounter in the form of the burning bush that was not consumed (see Exod. 3). This imagery draws attention to the divine imprint in every soul, the same inherent desire burning like fire and pushing us to search for the good, the beautiful, and the true.

Like the bush that was not consumed, the soul is not consumed by this divine fire; instead, it inspires us to ask for more, to draw closer to perfection, to want to embrace God and to be wrapped in His being. We want to possess God, to hold on to Him, and not to let Him depart from us. In each soul or heart is this fire, this push, this longing.

In the story of Moses, we see this chosen one thrilled by the sight. He drew nearer in either admiration, curiosity, or sheer wonder. Then from the thickest of the flames a unique voice spoke the name Yahweh—I AM. Observe the sequence of this revelation. First, there was a "fugitive," Moses, running away from the Pharaoh because of his love for his people, Israel. He is like any person on a wild search for the meaning of life; he was looking for answers to his life's journey. Humanity's ultimate search is for meaning, for no search is without a goal. *Ultimate meaning is life's natural elixir.* Finding it is the fulfillment of all desire. Not finding it is life's dreadful dirge.

Second, Moses' natural curiosity before the bush led him to contemplate the mystery that took place before him. He began a movement, drawing closer and closer to the light. He was, like many of us, a soul in search of the true light, the light of the world. But he was not worthy, as no one is worthy to step upon the terrace of the awe-inspiring presence of God, unless he removed his shoes. We should note the relevance of shoes in the ancient Near East: Without shoes, a traveler would hardly make it through the sunny, stony desert. You might call shoes an artificial support to a traveler's journey. But a time had come for Moses when physical shoes were not needed—when their use was subsumed by the power of God's grace. A time comes in our spiritual life when man-made support for our spiritual search gives way to the profundity of the divine embrace. We meet God as He has made us, without shoes, as God has purposed us for a blessed destiny. Isn't this the meaning of life we are searching for? Moses's experience captures what happens at the Beatific Vision, when we shall see God face-to-face and behold His glory.

Similarly, we arrive at the most profound revelation of the God-Moses encounter—the revelation of God's identity as "I AM," a name that at the same time is no name. For Moses, this too was beyond comprehension. The immanent God at the burning bush is at the same time the God of transcendence, the eternal "I AM." Moses learns that God is not like a king, whose name Pharaoh must know before he will liberate Israel. The name is for humans to accommodate the fact that we are limited by language; God is beyond a name or a concept.

Did Moses ever use "I AM" when Pharaoh asked, "Who sent you?" Never! He simply said, "The God of Israel sent me." He was bearing witness, proclaiming and testifying about the God in whom he believed. He didn't need to prove it anymore because Moses had witnessed the *theophany*—evidence based on God Himself. Once we meet God, only bearing witness to Him and proclaiming Him will do; argumentative proofs lose their luster. The life of faith has the perfect narrative of love, grace, and peace—not a feisty debate proposition—for its testimonial.

This divine revelation does not come easily. God's revelation of Himself at the beginning may not be clear to our minds because it may not follow the typical patterns of life we are accustomed to. After all, the Incarnation and the virginal birth are a clear sign that with God "all things are possible" (see Luke 18:27; Matt. 19:26). So God can do what He will. His ways may be totally different from what we expect or think. But the main issue is ascertaining with certainty that God has done something or said something—that is to say, that He has revealed His will.

If it is God, faith leads us to assent to its truth because God *is* truth.

But this awareness of divine revelation does not mean much if we do not respond to it. If we ignore it—if we go on living as if nothing has changed—it is a willful rejection of the true object of our ultimate search and desire, and is inconsistent with moral conduct. We have a right and a responsibility to the truth, to search for it and, ultimately, to abide by it when we find it. Thus, the revealed truth demands a response from us. This response is the fourth level of the journey where Christian spirituality develops in earnest.

Living the Christian Life

This last stage is what happens when we, like Moses, accept the revelation of God—you may also call it God's invitation—and allow it to influence and lead our lives. Simply put, it is when we enter into a relationship with God, become friends with Him, and live God-centered lives.

Here our knowledge is not only intellectual or mental, but also a living testimonial. We become part of the story of God's revelation because we have encountered God and bear witness to Him. Our life reflects God's glory. We know and choose to be influenced by what we know. We get to know God better and deeper and give our lives to Him in relationship. This relationship is of love and in love, for God is love.

Some may ask: Divine-human relationship? How is it possible? It is by the initiative of God Himself, who draws us into fellowship as he did with Moses at the burning bush. This, too, is the uniqueness of Judeo-Christian spirituality. God reveals Himself as a person—in the Son, Jesus Christ—to show us how to relate with Him as well as to give us the grace of incorporation into His Body, the grace of relationship. Thus, the life of faith is possible only by the grace of God.

We recall that Jesus said, "No one knows the Father except the Son and any one to whom the Son chooses to reveal Him" (Matt. 11:27). It is Jesus, the fullness of divine revelation, who leads us to this intimate relationship with God. The relationship is inspired, nourished, and sustained by the presence of the Holy Spirit within the Church, the Body of Christ. Then God's work becomes alive through sacred rites of worship — what in our Christian tradition we call the sacraments.

The Church presents us with two special case studies of people whose lives bear testimony to the journey of faith and the life of faith — Abraham and Mary. In the next two chapters, I will show how these two figures are each a model of the life of faith, lived in relationship with God. From their lives, I shall discuss the nature of faith, draw out some characteristics of faith, and show how the faith-life relationship with God is built, nourished, and grown. I will also show the challenges that the life of faith poses for believers on their faith journey.

Chapter 2

The Example of Abraham

Have you ever set out on a journey without really knowing where you were going? A pastor of a Catholic church in the United States made such a trip.

In 2009, a priest friend from Tanzania came to him in tears. His mother had died. A few days later, this generous pastor had packed for a journey to Tanzania to attend the funeral. He had never been to Africa and did not know that as an American, he would need a visa to enter Tanzania—plus he did not have the required malaria and yellow-fever vaccinations! He simply boarded an airplane and was off on his journey to help his friend. With layovers in Rome, Ethiopia, and Kenya, the trip took thirty-eight hours.

Of course, at customs in Tanzania this priest was denied entry to the country. When asked why he set out from America to a foreign country without a visa, he replied, "I just wanted to support this friend from Africa and to be by his side. I did not know what it entailed from an immigration point of view." It seemed like a joke to the agents. "Insanity!" they thought. Happily, though, the officials were able to streamline the process and get his immigration papers anyway.

Our Journey to God

When the priest arrived in the village, he had just a pair of jeans, two shirts, and a few dollars on him. He was surprised to find out just how different Tanzania is from America. The food was different. The climate was different. The people and their culture were different. Indeed, everything was different! He had started a journey that would change his views about other nations and would help him really understand all he had previously learned about faith in action.

He may have, in his little way, followed the example of Abraham by journeying to a foreign land because he believed God wanted him to do so. He heeded that first voice inspiring him to do something truly good while ignoring all the other voices that came after, trying to dissuade him. Many times, the faith journey requires listening to that first voice.

The story of Abraham is popular in most African countries thanks to the widespread growth of Christianity across the continent. Many preachers want to talk about Abraham; after all, his story is rich with material for sermons. In fact, there is a song that is popular in many West African countries called "Abraham's Blessings Are Mine." Many like to sing this song and to appropriate "in faith" the blessings of Abraham, which the Bible says belong to all believers. But not many dig deeper to know what Abraham did for God that led him to be so abundantly blessed. The faith journey of Abraham is a good model for us to reflect on.

The blessings promised to Abraham were twofold: First, he will be blessed and, second, he will be a blessing. Becoming a blessing, it seems to me, goes even deeper than being blessed. When a person is a beneficiary of divine favors, that person is said to be blessed by God. These blessings may include excellent health, a good and happy family, an amazing spouse, wonderful

The Example of Abraham

and healthy children, a nice job, and spiritual satisfactions such as peace and happiness. But if the beneficiary of these favors keeps them within himself and fails to share them, they may not be a blessing to others.

To be a blessing is to become a channel of grace and favor to other people; it is when other people are blessed *through you*. I'll bet many of us would like not only to be blessed but also to become a conduit for blessing others. In this chapter, we are going to explore how the faith journey of Abraham made him both blessed *and* a blessing for generations to come.

Scripture tells us a few things about Abraham's background but much more about his journey of faith. Born in the pagan land of Ur, he was probably a farmer. He was depicted as constantly on the go—to wherever God wanted him to be. His life was a typical example of a faith journey—not just intellectually, but truly a journey to many places around the ancient Near East—as can be seen throughout the book of Genesis. For the purposes of our reflections, let us look closely at two texts—Genesis 12:1–3 and 22:1–3—that, in addition to telling Abraham's story, have a Christological message.

Genesis 12 introduces us to the story of Abram's first encounter with God ("Abraham" was the expanded name given to him by God):

> Now the Lord said to Abram, "Go from your country and your kindred and your father's house to the land that I will show you. And I will make of you a great nation, and I will bless you, and make your name great, so that you will be a blessing. I will bless those who bless you, and him who curses you I will curse; and by you all the families of the earth shall bless themselves." (Gen. 12:1–3)

Abram set out from the land of Ur to the land of the un-known. He wandered through the desert until he became tired and rested under the oak of Mamre. There God appeared to him and said, "To your descendants I give this land" (Gen. 15:18).

Abraham's wandering is a prototype of any faith journey, when we wander through our own lives grappling with the precarious and unpredictable nature of our voyage. In the faith journey, although we may be certain of our eternal destination, we abso-lutely do not know where we are on the path to that destination; that judgment belongs to God. There are gray areas that God allows so that we will realize we do not and cannot completely comprehend Him. This keeps us humble and on track toward the goal for which we have been made. As the mystic St. Catherine of Siena describes it, God is like the deep sea in which the more we seek, the more we find—and the more we find, the more we seek. The faith journey must come to terms with the reality that God is close yet cannot be fully grasped.

Now, suppose you are sleeping or relaxing in your backyard and a surprising and unique voice speaks to you, saying, "Get up and go to a land I will show you. There I will make you prosper-ous." You get up and tell your wife, "Honey, we are going to sell our house, liquidate our savings, cash in our retirement, and head in a direction unknown, to follow God's will which He will reveal once we are on our way." Your wife, without hesitation, supports you and follows you on this journey to the unknown, based on your claim of a revelation. Wow, she must be a special woman of faith!

If this incident happened in Africa, where you would also have to tell all your extended family, it would be an ordeal to convince them you aren't losing it! They would grill you: Where exactly are you going? What exactly inspired your sudden decision to relocate? Have you mapped it out with a GPS? If you answer that you do not know where you are going, so you can't map it out, and that you will be *guided* to where you are supposed to go once you leave, your family really will think you have lost it. As for your wife, they may accuse her of supporting your daydreaming.

A literal reading of the story of Abraham might look like the picture presented above, and could even be dismissed by skeptics as a narrative about lunatics who hear voices and lack common sense. But let's instead look at this narrative with the eyes of faith.

In the story of Abraham and his wife, God reaches out to His creatures to introduce them to true worship and to dissuade them from the idolatrous practices of the land of Ur. The supernatural meeting at Mamre was not a mere voice or a dream but a unique revelation, which has a divine seal as evidence. Subsequent events were proofs of its uniqueness: Israel would come to know God, who is both the Creator and the Liberator—a personal God more than a mere force in the cosmos. Indeed, without Abraham's encounter, the religions of "the Book" (Judaism, Christianity, Islam, also known as the Abrahamic faiths) would not have been born.

Let's turn now to another crucial moment when God put Abraham's faith to the test. This second example is also prone to many criticisms by skeptics, but again it has lessons beyond mere face level. Here is the setting:

> After these things God tested Abraham, and said to him, "Abraham!" And he said, "Here am I." He said "Take your son, your only begotten son Isaac, whom you love, and go to the land of Moriah, and offer him there as a burnt offering upon one of the mountains of which I shall tell

you. So Abraham rose early in the morning, saddled his donkey, and took two of his young men with him, and his son Isaac; and he cut the wood for the burnt offering, and arose and went to the place of which God had told him. (Gen. 22:1–3)

After almost seventy childless years, God finally fulfills His promise and grants Abraham a miraculous son — and then asks Abraham to offer up this child as a sacrifice. This sounds strange, doesn't it? Taken out of context, it might even sound savage. Again, though, with the eyes of faith we can see the spiritual significance of the demand God made on Abraham. God never actually intended for Abraham to kill his son; He already had a plan to stop this from happening. Rather, the test was to determine Abraham's ultimate loyalty: Was it to God, or to his own legacy?

These two instances have much to show us about the nature and challenges of faith. Observe that God spoke in similar terms and called on Abraham to make a decision based on two sorts of commands: Go[5] (or, similarly, move or leave) and take.[6] The journey of faith begins with God directing us to change a course of action — and the very course of our lives. It is then up to us to respond. Faith, therefore, develops in the form of a dialogue.

---

[5] The Hebrew is הָלַךְ (pronounced halak), meaning "to go." We can understand it broadly as "leaving for a new location." The idea of a traveler, a sojourner, or a wayfarer, which this word also relates to in Hebrew, is evident. Abraham is a sojourner just as all believers are sojourners — pilgrims to where God leads.

[6] The Hebrew is חָקַל (pronounced lawkákh) meaning "to take," "to grasp," or "to receive." It suggests an intentional act.

The Example of Abraham

Faith as a Dialogue

In terms of God and humans, faith is a two-way interaction — a dialogue. On the one hand, there are the truths we are to believe; this is called *objective faith*. On the other hand is our assent to those truths, which is called *subjective faith*. The objective faith could be called *the Faith* and the subjective faith, simply, *faith*. When people say, "This is my faith" or "This is our faith," they are likely referring to objective faith. When they say, "I believe" or "I have faith," they are probably alluding to subjective faith. The two are not opposites, of course, but are interwoven in the life of one who is journeying in faith.

As we have said, faith begins with revelation — that is, God revealing Himself. This revelation is a divine intervention in human history so as to draw humanity to the knowledge of God. This revelation, therefore, demands a response, and it is this response that completes the faith dialogue. God reveals; we consent to the revelation.

Faith is objective (*fides quae*, or "faith which," as it is called in academic theology) because there are truths that God has revealed that demand our assent. These truths are objective — that is, their truth is not relative to any person, experience, or circumstance — and are held by the Church as divine revelation. In the context of Christian worship, therefore, they are also ecclesial — that is, related directly to the life of the Church.

Faith is subjective (*fides qua*, or "faith by which," as theologians say) because it requires the assent of the individual to those objective truths — the *faith by which* a person is moved to respond to God. This is subjective because it includes a person's own understanding of his relationship to God, which is different from every other person's experience. It is our saying yes instead of no to God with our heart, our intellect, and our will, and thereby receiving God Himself. It is the subject (an individual, such as Abraham, Mary, and I) who makes this assent of faith that allows his life to be turned around and that leads to salvation. As Pope Benedict XVI expressed, Christian faith engages the individual in a "constant and committed assent of the revealed truth."[7]

In Abraham, these two aspects of faith blended in perfect order. Quite simply he believed (subjective faith) God's word (objective faith). This was credited to him as righteousness (Gen. 15:6; Rom. 4:3, 22). By believing, a new life is weaved — the life of faith. This life is made righteous because it is lived by faith in God.

Hence, we see in condensed form a summary of revelation, as well as the Christian thesis of justification in Christ. When we believe God's revelation and respond to it through the obedience of faith, we receive divine justification. The dialogue implies the action of two responsible persons: one divine, the other human; one the giver, the other the receiver; one the justifier, the other the justified. The genesis and consummation of faith leading to

---

[7] Benedict XVI, Encyclical Letter *Spe salvi* (*Saved in Hope*), November 30, 2007, no. 7. The Holy Father also shows how the Faith draws the future closer to us. "Faith is not merely a personal reaching out towards things to come that are still totally absent: it gives us something. It gives us even now something of the reality we are waiting for, and this present reality constitutes for us a 'proof' of the things that are still unseen. Faith draws the future into the present, so that it is no longer simply a 'not yet.' The fact that this future exists changes the present; the present is touched by the future reality, and thus the things of the future spill over into those of the present and those of the present into those of the future." Ibid., no. 7.

the justification of the believer in Christ is God's initiative. Nevertheless, between the genesis and the consummation, there is yet the action of the human person whose obedience and "work of faith," as St. Paul calls it (1 Thess. 1:3), realize the benefits of the faith in his life. We call this faith lived in works of charity.

Similarly, faith as a two-way interaction relates to prayer, which is itself a dialogue. Assent to divine revelation implies not just an intellectual response but acts of gratitude, prayer, and worship. Faith and prayer, therefore, are like two sides of a coin. You cannot be a person of prayer unless you are a person of faith, just as you cannot claim to be a person of faith if you are not a person of prayer.

In the life of Abraham, we see that faith and prayer go together. His life of prayer was expressed in the Genesis account through acts of worship and sacrifice. Abraham offered personal sacrifices to the Lord, and built three altars for the Lord. He built one of the altars at Schechem (Gen. 12:6–7), which means "shoulder" or "a place to carry our burdens." Some Bible scholars see this as a sign of personal prayer—a petition for help from God; hence, the altar is regarded as the altar of personal prayer. Recall that it was at Schechem where Jacob discarded all the idols on his way to Bethel (Gen. 35:4).

Abraham built the second altar at Bethel (Gen. 12:8; 13:4), regarded as the "House of God." Some people see this altar as one of ecclesial worship. The last altar built by Abraham was at Hebron—meaning "alliance" (Gen. 13:18). Later David was to start his ministry at Hebron, which is the highest place in Israel. Abraham built these three altars to mark God's encounter with him and in gratitude to God for His revelations. These two devotions—personal sacrifices and building altars—were unique Old Testament gestures demonstrating a deep prayer life.

In Hebrew *altar* means "place of slaughter"[8] or "a place for the offering of slain animals," and it was first mentioned in biblical history in Genesis 8:20–22, when Noah built "an altar for burnt sacrifice, to thank the Lord for gracious protection, and pray for His mercy in time to come."[9] In Greek it means "a place for sacrifice." Abraham's faith was also related to sacrifice because he was willing to offer back to God the gifts he had been given.

Look at the symbolism of these three places where Abraham built the altars: names referencing sacrifice, the house of God, and alliance. The symbolic implication of these places could be that Abraham offered a sacrifice to God (prayer), built Him a house ("my house shall be called a house of prayer for all peoples" [Isa. 56:7]), and pledged his total alliance to the Lord. In simple terms, Abraham's journey of faith portrays a response of reciprocal obedience to the divine invitation by prayer and sacrifice.

Faith Requires Our Reciprocal Obedience

Faith is an invitation advanced by God. When we do not honor the invitation by responding to it with reciprocal obedience, then, while the objective substance of faith remains, the subjective

---

[8]   Altars were built by Noah after leaving the ark (Gen. 8:20); by Abraham at Shechem (Gen. 12:7), Bethel (Gen. 12:8), Hebron (Gen. 13:8), and Moriah (Gen. 22:9); by Isaac at Beersheba (Gen. 26:25); by Jacob at Shechem (Gen. 33:20) and Bethel (Gen. 35:7); by Moses at Rephidim (Exod. 17:15) and Horeb (Exod. 24:4); by Balak at Bamoth Baal, Pisgah, and Peor (Num. 23:1, 14, 29); by Joshua on Mount Ebal (Josh. 8:30); and so forth.

[9]   C. F. Keil and F. Delitzsch, *Commentary on the Old Testament*, vol. 1 (Peabody, MA: Hendrickson, 1996), 95.

appreciation is lacking. In the journey of faith, God sets the vision, and we respond to that vision. For a person of faith, concern for God, His words, and His revelations becomes the objects of primary concern. Divine wish is literally understood as divine command because a person of faith perceives that God's wish for us is identical with God's plan, will, and action. We use the word *perceive* because, while imperfect, it is the closest word to describe how the soul grasps this divine revelation.

In both his wandering and his willingness to sacrifice his son, Abraham was directed by God to do what by human understanding was outrageously unpopular and impractical. Abraham understood, though, that respectability does not necessarily mean divine acceptance. He understood that with human beings, what seems wise might be foolish by God's standard, for man's wisdom is foolishness before God. To leave your place of comfort and security to go to an unknown fantasy world is, in worldly terms, unacceptable. The test of faith confronts one of our most basic instincts: security, which draws from the basic instinct of self-preservation.

I recently read about the experiences of the early Christians during the persecutions of the first three centuries of the Church. Among the key strategies used to compel a number of Christians to deny their Faith was to strike at their need for financial security. The book of Job shows that the tempter believed Job was faithful to God because he was financially secure. The tempter assumed that without this security, Job would never be a believer. We see this line of thought commonly among people today. One of the greatest obstacles to faith for people who lack financial stability is to have a paycheck dangled in front of their face with a bold tag: "Can your *so-called God* provide you with a job or with money?" Economic power is employed by those in positions of authority to shake the very foundation of the faith of the less powerful and well-off.

In the United States, the power of the Internal Revenue Service, for instance, could easily become corrupted with respect to religious organizations who wish to teach the truth *and* to preserve their tax-exempt status as nonprofits. A well-intended policy designed to protect nonprofits may have the unintended consequence of giving powerful forces sway over such organizations.

Other examples include cases in which an organization or government threatens to end a business relationship or the provision of aid to try to compel assent to particular points of view. The abortion agenda, for instance, has been pushed in Africa by some in the West under subtle threats of economic sanctions. In other words, money is being used to proselytize for secular progressivism — and against the freedom of the often-powerless people of Africa. Those of little faith fall for it — the allure of the dollar is strong. It should be no surprise that our Savior, Jesus Christ, was tempted by the devil with food and worldly possessions.

Once I received a letter from a Christian who said it was impossible for him to keep trusting or even believing in God when God did not seem to answer his prayers for financial security. I led him through prayers, reassuring him of God's abiding love and providence. His was on a long journey of ups and downs, but thanks be to God he came away from it stronger in faith and full of joy in the Lord — where true security lies. Shakespeare writes in *Macbeth*, "Security is mortals' chiefest enemy." Temptations to disbelieve because of our insecurities — financial, medical, psychological, and so on — can be daunting, but with faith in God and His grace, we can overcome.

The greatest challenge to faith in Africa is poverty. How can one believe in the God of the Cross, when there are many voices that speak from the traditional cults with assurances of a magical breakthrough? Who does not wish, at some point or another, for a cheap financial jackpot? We must be wary of movies and films that depict cheap popularity and easy success. This is not the way of faith. Take the example of Abraham and learn to move by faith, for Scripture says, "My righteous one shall live by faith" (Heb. 10:38).

Faith does not promise financial breakthroughs or a magical transformation of stone into bread or dry land into ocean. Faith does not promise blessings without effort; it does not assure us of eternal sunshine, because nature needs nighttime too. Instead, faith enables us to make the best of every moment and leads us along the path of divine blessedness with the constant assurance of ultimate peace and happiness. Faith, in effect, gives us a true and divine security that may manifest itself in many forms — spiritual and temporal. That is, even if our prayers don't lead to a big raise or some other windfall, our reliance on God will bring an even more important spiritual security. Abraham's faith reassures us about the kind of security that endures; he gladly gives up everything that prevents him from entrusting his future to God's blessed assurance.

Intercession as a Sign of Growth in Faith

God appeared to or spoke to Abraham three times (Gen. 12:1–3, 7; 13:14–17), but Abraham *never asked God anything*. This was one of my newest discoveries as I reread the book of Genesis recently. Abraham simply did exactly what the Lord wanted, with no questions asked and no clarifications sought. *He simply obeyed*. This was incredible faith coming from somebody who had never heard of or known the true God.

Remember the significance of the number three in our Judeo-Christian tradition. Not only does this number remind us of the Trinity, but it's a sign of completeness and communion. The first three encounters between God and Abraham, we notice, were all about God. Abraham was like a child following the lead of his heavenly Father. Recall that during the course of these first three encounters, many things happened in the life of Abraham that would have made almost any other person object to God's call and revelation. These included his experience in Egypt (Gen. 12) and the dispute about the land between his herdsmen and those of Lot, his nephew, which led to Lot's parting with him (Gen. 13). It wasn't until the fourth visit of God that Abraham first made a petition to God. Otherwise, he simply obeyed, built an altar to the Lord, and worshipped. This is important in the life of faith. The constant awareness of God's will and the willingness to trust God is key to faith.

Let us look now at how Abraham's faith grew to intercession. According to the contemporary Jewish Scripture scholar Nahum Sarna, the first three times Abraham spoke to God (Gen. 15:2, 8; 17:17), "his personal welfare has been the sole subject of discourse." Starting in Genesis 18, however, we see a change in the story. "The next dialogue with God involves a concern for the welfare of others, total strangers. Abraham displays an awareness of suffering and an ability to respond beyond his immediate personal interests. He shows himself to be a moral and compassionate man. His behavior at this moment makes him the paradigm of 'the just and the right,' qualities that are to characterize his descendants."[10]

---

[10] Nahum M. Sarna, *Genesis* (Philadelphia: Jewish Publication Society, 1989), 132–134. See Gen. 18:18.

The Example of Abraham

It's beautiful to see how Abraham goes beyond himself—and the concerns of both his immediate family and his tribe—to intercede for the people of Sodom and Gomorrah, who were regarded as pagans. His prayer wasn't necessarily for their conversion, or even their repentance. (Such a concept had yet to be understood by the people of his time; rather it was a later revelation starting from the story of Jonah and the rest of the prophets.) Abraham's interest was about tempering God's justice with mercy.

His faith as an intercessor teaches us many things. First, our faith life should help us grow beyond our personal interests to concern for others' welfare, and from justice to mercy and compassion. Abraham did not *need* to pray for God to stop the destruction of Sodom and Gomorrah on account of the innocence of a few. The people of those cities were not in any way related to him. Yet he became their intercessor. Likewise, Abraham's faith triumphed over the natural human temptation to revenge, despite the greed of Lot, who chose the better side of the fields for his flock, relegating Abraham to the rocky, unfertile land. The part that Lot chose, it turned out, was the locale of the destruction, but Abraham overlooked Lot's treachery and continued to intercede for him and the rest of the people of Sodom and Gomorrah.

Similarly, his faith had already helped him to *trust* that the true God isn't simply a God of justice but also a God of compassion and mercy. This second aspect of his intercessory role is groundbreaking and, as Sarna suggests, carries with it two implications: "Indirectly it asserts that there is a greater infraction of justice in the death of an innocent few than in allowing a guilty majority to escape retribution; it assumes that the merit of a minority is powerful enough to overcome the wickedness of the majority."[11]

---

[11] Ibid.

Know this: *Your faith-filled prayers for those in need of divine mercy aren't simply a footnote in the life of faith.* They may start out as a small part of your prayer life, but they should always be increasing in fervor and intensity if they are to fulfill God's will as Abraham's efforts did.

Between the Faith and Security

Faith required Abraham to hand over his security — the Land of Ur, where he was born and where he was assured of the comfort of the wealth of his father, and Isaac, the child of the promise, who would guarantee the future of his progeny. What God was demanding was a life totally lived by faith.

How could Abraham do this when there was no physical evidence that this was God speaking to him? Abraham's only evidence — which for a person who is not open to divine insight is foolishness — was his intuition that the voice he heard was God's; and if it was God, then His words must be true. And so he believed; he decided; and he acted. In the end, Abraham was justified, for God is always true.

Abraham believed God, and this was credited to him as righteousness (see Gal. 3:6; James 2:23). Did this mean Abraham had to keep his fingers crossed and do nothing? Was his faith merely an intellectual assent without any sort of action to back it up? Far from it! We know much about Abraham's faith not simply because of his mental acceptance of revelation, but because he acted upon it by moving to the place of promise that God offered to give him. The example of faith he gave for generations to come was both intellectual and volitional: He believed, chose to act, and acted. This is essential: Christian faith is not a mere knowledge of God or of God's presence in our lives. This aspect of the Christian faith is *necessary* but not *sufficient*; it does not lead to a life lived in faith, nor to a transforming relationship with God and with other people. This transforming power requires action.

In fact, the ethical demands of Christian faith are explicit about responsibility and a good work ethic, built on the dignity of labor for human well-being and security. Abraham did his part. Sometimes the actions required of us may seem revolutionary, but so long as they give glory to God and promote the common good in defense of life, justice, and truth, they are testimony to faith's audacity. Faith, we have seen, has a unique boldness to it.

To live a life of faith, for instance, means that a religious person in Africa should speak and act against the corruption that has made so much of the continent poor, and it means that a believer in the West should work for the reign of justice in the world and defend true human freedom. The life of faith involves the pew and the desk, the chapel and the workplace, the catechism class and the street. It is a responsible blend of what we believe and the life we lead outside the places we specifically call sacred.

In essence, faith demands us to confront evil and to live the truth. Faith, therefore, is another way of describing a divinely approved responsibility. Faith demands action — a work that is its clear proof before skeptics. James says, "Show me your faith apart from your works, and I by my works will show you my faith" (James 2:18). If the Christian faith is losing its saltiness and its sweetness in our contemporary world, it is because believers have disconnected what they believe from the way they act by unnaturally separating faith and life.

Faith requires us to go and to take — to leave our comfort zone to go where God wants us to be and to take what we think is too precious to give up and offer it up to God, who "shall provide." We are to leave old habits and to take up obedience to God's command, completely trusting in the God of revelation, our Lord Jesus Christ, who is the fullness of divine revelation. Like Abraham, we offer up to God our most cherished gifts upon "the mountain of God's plan" so that we can get down to the field of divine acceptance. We allow our lives to be transformed by what we believe so we can put those beliefs into action in our daily lives for the glory of God and for the salvation of many.

Chapter 3

The Example of Mary

In the Gospel of Luke we read:

> In the sixth month the angel Gabriel was sent from God
> to a city of Galilee named Nazareth, to a virgin betrothed
> to a man whose name was Joseph, of the house of David;
> and the virgin's name was Mary. And he came to her and
> said, "Hail, full of grace, the Lord is with you!" But she
> was greatly troubled at the saying, and considered in her
> mind what sort of greeting this might be. And the angel
> said to her, "Do not be afraid, Mary, for you have found
> favor with God. And behold, you will conceive in your
> womb and bear a son, and you shall call his name Jesus. . . .
> And Mary said, "Behold, I am the handmaid of the Lord;
> let it be to me according to your word." And the angel
> departed from her. (Luke 1:26–31, 38)

This is the mystery of the Annunciation, when a young woman's
assent of faith ushered in the greatest event in human history: the
Incarnation — God taking flesh — so as to save us from sin and
invite us to the richness of God's love. From this mystery, we can
see another account of the journey of faith. As Abraham was the

male prototype of faith, Mary is regarded as the female prototype of faith because she said the yes by which God became man.

The Acceptance of the Person of God

Christian faith is primarily about accepting the person of our Lord and Savior Jesus Christ. This reality enables us to relate to God as a person—a being with whom we can enter into a relationship. Moreover, Christian faith is about a relationship with all three persons in one God—the Father, the Son, and the Holy Spirit—and the way to this relationship is modeled after Christ, the Son, who is fully divine *and* fully human. Our faith is not a belief in some special force, energy, or vague cosmic power. Christian faith, rather, acknowledges that there is life beyond the forces of nature and that "oneness" with the forces of nature is not and cannot be the goal of our religious aspirations.

Christian faith believes in real persons who transcend space and time: the Person of Jesus, God the Son, the Person of God the Father, and the Person of the Holy Spirit. Together these three Persons are one personal God, the Trinity who shapes all things and who orders nature. The way to this Trinitarian faith is *through* the Son *by the power of* the Holy Spirit; hence, Christian faith is Christocentric—centered in Christ as the fullness of God's revelation.[12]

Mary is the paradigm for complete acceptance of the persons of the Trinitarian God. She would have had no frame of reference

---

[12] Christian faith is not a belief in the person of any minister, bishop, priest, pastor, prophet, visionary, wonder-worker, or whoever else might elicit religious excitement, no matter how holy or powerful that person may seem. We must resist the temptation to confuse the faith with the minister.

for understanding the Trinity, but she was so imbued with God's grace that she instantly accepted the word of God the Father (the first Person) that she would conceive His Son (the second Person) by the power of the Holy Spirit (the third Person). Her response, "Be it done to me according to your word," remains a model of Christian faith.

While I was ministering in Nigeria, I found that sometimes people built their faith around *me* as a spiritual leader to the point that it might have become idolatrous. I have observed similar temptations among many influential pastors and evangelizers all over the world. Making sure the attention goes to God is sometimes a challenge for believers—and especially for leaders. This was one of the challenges Paul faced in Lystra, when the Lycaonians, seeing the great miracles God did through him, thought of him as Hermes and thought of Barnabas, his companion, as Zeus. They said, "The Gods have come down to us in the likeness of men!" (Acts 14:11).

When the faith of a worshipping community is based on the prowess of the minister, the community's faith is on the thin ice of human respect, always in danger of collapsing into idolatry. Have we not seen many move from faith to disappointment in a church minister who causes a scandal, then to a loss of confidence in the Church as a whole, and finally to a loss of faith in God? I can't say it enough: *Placing ultimate faith in human beings is idolatrous.*

If you find yourself moving from one church to another, ask yourself why. If the reason is the person of the minister, then you must be careful. The Catholic Church wisely teaches that the sacraments act *ex opere operato*, that is, they are efficacious because of the work of Christ, and do not depend on the holiness of the minister, provided that he does what the Church intends for that sacrament.

Similarly, Christian faith is not, as some modern preachers teach, a self-confident belief in oneself that will allow us to achieve impossible feats. Although a sense of optimism is often experienced by the faithful, true faith is not optimism in what *I* can do. Rather, faith is optimism in what Jesus Christ has revealed, done, and could do *in me* and *through me* on the one hand and, on the other hand, what Jesus did and does in and through His Body, the Church. It is about Jesus, not about me; it is about God's grace, not about my power. Mary's phrase "Behold the handmaid of the Lord," expresses and acknowledges this God-based sense of both optimism and resignation.

A Life of Gratitude

Recall from the last chapter the connection between faith and prayer in the life of Abraham. In the life of Mary we see another form of the lived response to faith: a life lived in gratitude to God. Faith in God is the vehicle for gratitude to the Source of our life and existence. The Canticle of Mary, known in the Catholic tradition as the Magnificat (Luke 1:46–55), summarizes this thankful response of faith. A faith-inspired life of gratitude takes a communal turn when the assembly of God unites to celebrate the Eucharist, "the source and summit of ecclesial life."[13]

In the Liturgy of the Eucharist, we are grateful (*eukharistos*) and so we offer thanksgiving (*eukharistia*) to God for the sacrifice that His Son made once and for all on the Cross for our salvation. Mary followed Jesus along the road to Calvary and was present at the foot of the Cross to witness His last breath that was offered

---

[13] Vatican Council II, Dogmatic Constitution on the Church *Lumen gentium*, November 21, 1964, no.11. See also CCC 1324.

for our salvation. The life of faith is a life of gratitude because the faithful realize that life is a gift, faith in God is a gift, and the fulfillment of our desires is a gift—and all of these gifts come from God. No matter what we face in life, faith helps us to see the good in all things and to be grateful in all things.

The practice of celebrating a special thanksgiving holiday emerges from the idea of gratitude to the Provider. In most churches in Africa, communities celebrate the harvest thanksgiving by replicating the Aramaic/Jewish practice of Deuteronomy 26. They offer to the Lord the fruits of their labor in appreciation for the gifts of life, rain, sunshine, the moon, the stars, and, of course, the harvest. For most churches in Africa the harvest becomes a collective thanksgiving to God and a testimony of the faith of the people. Gratitude that does not recognize the giver of the gift becomes self-congratulations—the springboard of narcissism. Faith, on the other hand, helps us to reach beyond ourselves and to appreciate what we have been given. It heals us from excessive self-centeredness.

The second aspect of thanksgiving is that it diffuses to others, leading them to experience joy. Mary embodies this as well. Her faithful and gracious voice made the baby John the Baptist in the womb of Elizabeth leap for joy. Her greetings also inspired Elizabeth to shout in praise of God. The faith example of Mary is a catalyst for gratitude and praise in others. The life of faith—and the spirit of gratitude that comes with it—should therefore be an inspiration to others.

This social aspect of faith shows us that our relationship with God is not *just* private. Instead, faith is an integral part of the Christian life, shaping the way the believer talks, works, and relates with others. If I believe in God, then people should be able to see in me a correlation with the God in whom I believe.

Jesus said, "Let your light so shine before men, that they may see your good works and give glory to your Father who is in heaven" (Matt. 5:16). He could have said, "Let the people see your *faith* and give glory to your father in heaven," but He did not.

The life of faith is seen by others in the way the believer lives. One of the marks of such a faith-filled life is that it should resonate with joy, peace, gracefulness, gratitude, and service. If the way a Christian lives does not make people glad to be around him, then he isn't witnessing to Christ. Once a woman told me about her abusive father, who she said was more religious than any man she had ever known. But whenever this man came home from work, everyone in the house became tense. He carried an air of unhappiness all the time. The daughter complained that his presence made her sad and depressed. "I wonder how I will serve the same God that my father serves," she said to me.

Compare this story with another shared by one of my Nigerian friends who is an entrepreneur. One day he entered a shop owned by a Muslim and, after pricing some goods, found he could not afford them. He politely thanked the shopkeeper and left. The next week, he passed the same shop. The shopkeeper called out to him with great excitement and said, "Friend, come into my shop. I am satisfied if you choose not to buy anything; just come in. The other day you came in here, and your presence brought so much joy, peace, and happiness to me, which I had never witnessed before. Ever since, I am a happy salesman, and this has even affected my returns, which have improved exponentially." The young man said to him, "Well, I am a man of faith in God and His Christ, and that is likely why my life has so much joy as to impact yours. Thank you for your kind words." Faith is a catalyst for affecting those around us and society at large.

The Example of Mary

I had the opportunity to work at a parish in California in 2015. This parish grew from 1,500 registered families to about 8,000 in less than seventeen years. While many churches of all denominations in the United States are losing membership, this church is growing every day. During my first month in the church, I wanted to figure out why it was growing rapidly. One of the major reasons shared by the parishioners is the joy that flows from the pastor and his associates to the people, and vice versa. And the foundation of their joy and hospitality is a spirit of gratitude to God. The sacramental practices of the congregation are very encouraging, and the church is full to capacity for Mass. Their joy, peace, and praise of God are palpable—a sweet nectar to many souls.

A Life of Service

In the life of Mary we also see how faith translates into service. Like Abraham, when Mary believed, she acted. It's impossible to name a holy man or woman in Scripture or in the history of the Church whose faith was not matched with a life of service. Even hermits and abbots who lived in caves devoted ceaseless hours to prayer for the welfare of the world. Why? Because their faith had become the very core of their existence, so much so that it expressed itself in love and service. Faith at its best is married to love, and the source of all love is God. A deeper life of faith is absorbed in the absolute love of God, and love of neighbor for the sake of God. Prayer and action can always go together and support each other.

Christian faith has the capacity of healing the wounds of separation between people. It pulls down the dividing wall and its antecedent hatred. In the existential, sociological sense, an authentic faith blurs the distinction between ethnic, racial, class, sex, and cultural barriers, for it sees the neighbor as a person cre- ated in the image and likeness of God. Since God is the ultimate concern of the faithful, the neighbor is appreciated in terms of his ultimate identity as one of God's creatures. Christian faith unites and should therefore not divide. Thus, it is a false faith that, instead of promoting love and service of neighbor, engages in acts of violence in the name of religion. Violence in the name of religion negates the very nature of authentic faith, namely, service of God and neighbor.

Total Submission to God's Will

Faith is a life lived in total submission to God's will, even when His plans could lead to ridicule and ostracism. Mary was open to the Cross, which always looms over the life of faith. She was a young girl who conceived by the power of the Holy Spirit and managed a pregnancy that she, before the Annunciation, never would have thought would be her calling. And yet she lived this difficult, even frightening life with courage and graciousness.

There is a subtlety I want to draw our attention to here that is easy to ignore. What happens when faith demands that we make a choice between two acts that are both morally good but only one, the more challenging between them, is God's will for us? God asked for Mary's yes for the consummation of the mystery of the Incarnation. Mary submitted to the will of the Father, whom she loved and worshipped in spite of a personal commitment to virginity, a holy gift, which by human calculation excludes the possibility of childbirth. It reveals how her mind had been always attuned to the will of her Father. Faith in the divine will required Mary to leave her comfort zone as a young girl in Nazareth who evidently was not thinking of being a mother, to become not just any mother, but the mother of the Savior. This, for an average girl, would be a tough pill to swallow. But because she obeyed, "all generations shall call [her] blessed" (Luke 1:48).

This aspect of the mystery of the Incarnation may appear easy to many. After all, who would not accept the invitation to be the mother of the Savior of the world? But in real life, this is not how matters of faith evolve. Hindsight is a tricky tool, because it blurs the risks and uncertainties that are all too apparent in the present. Just think about how, to this day, an "unplanned pregnancy" is one of the greatest fears of young people. If we were to go back to Nazareth at the time of the Incarnation, we would appreciate that there was nothing easy about accepting this invitation simply on the word of an angel called Gabriel. But Mary said yes, because her lifelong experience with God was defined by "yes." Yes to the will of God. Yes to God's plan.

In the here and now, sometimes what the Church asks of us may not be very comfortable for us. Sometimes the Faith may require us to be silent when we would have loved to sing aloud and dance to God. Other times, we may desire to become a priest or a religious, but by listening to the voice of God, we see that our vocation is to married life instead. Or it could be the other way around. What may be comfortable might not be the will of God. This is the scary part—the will of God is not always pleasant by our human reckoning. In fact, its constant companion is the Cross. The further you are from the Cross, the more likely you are making the wrong choice. Mary's yes drew the Holy Family closer to the Cross, for without the Annunciation and the Incarnation, there would not have been the Crucifixion.

Sometimes our faith in God challenges us to turn our cheek to an enemy. Sometimes it requires us to forgive the person who has committed the most painful sins against those closest to us. The Faith requires us not to take up arms in revenge against a terrorist who has killed our relatives in cold blood at a church service in Kenya, Southern Sudan, northern Nigeria, Somalia, or Uganda—or in the United States. Self-defense is different from vengeance; true faith resists vengeance. Yes, it's often difficult not to pay back violent acts against us. Faith often takes its holy toll upon us, but it requires the constant yes to God's will, not our desires, to live the faith we profess and to grow in that divine relationship with Him.

It takes faith in God to bring about things that never could have been. Faith helps us to connect the dots between the natural and the supernatural. It is by faith that we understand God's plan in our lives and in society and become ready to submit to it.

And Mary, the Mother of God, embodied this complete faith by her life of gratitude and service in total submission to God's will. She is our example of faith. Let us always strive to respond to God's will as Mary did: "Be it done to me according to your word."

Chapter 4

Faith and Doubt

There was a great spiritual reawakening throughout West Africa right after the Second Vatican Council, especially from the late seventies through the early nineties. Testimonies of revival, God's healing hands, blossoming faith, miracles, and deep love for the Lord were widespread. God did incredible things among His people, and the rapid growth of faith we see in the region today is likely the fruit of that period.

Truly, West African was in need. Many communities were divided between allegiance to the Christian faith and allegiance to their ancestral cults (gathered under the heading of African Traditional Religions). The eighties and the nineties were the critical turning point, and God graced the time with many signs and wonders to draw people to faith in Christ. Massive conversions were recorded. Grace is real, and God responds to our needs.

But the blessings of those days were not without problems. We know very well from spiritual warfare that the enemy is closest where God's grace is abundant. Bible stories show that the enemy has a pattern of posing counterfeits in response to authentic divine miracles or special moments of grace. We saw it in the ministry of our Lord when, after He had fasted for forty days and forty nights, the devil was on hand to test Him. The pattern was the same with the Transfiguration. While the three apostles closest to Jesus (Peter, James, and John) witnessed the great manifestation of the Transfiguration, beneath the mountain the devil was showing the weakness of Jesus' disciples in their inability to drive out demons. Examples like this are numerous in the Bible, and they continue in our time. The growth of faith in Africa after the Second Vatican Council is no exception.

Basking in religious excitement, some zealous believers made the quest for signs and wonders the entirety of their "faith." Stories abound of the paradoxes of those moments. Take, for instance, a story about a young girl who was said to have encountered the Lord through what is called in the charismatic movement a "baptism of the Holy Spirit." The zealous girl, motivated by the word of the Lord as recorded in Matthew 17:20,[14] asked for the gift of faith, the kind that moves mountains. She felt her prayers were answered but needed proof to validate her claim; therefore, she set a date. The girl fasted for days and nights, waiting for the day to demonstrate her faith in God. And finally it came.

She invited her siblings to come over, and, to their utter surprise, she started to pray over a dead grasshopper, invoking it in the name of the Lord to come back to life. She explained: "God promised that if I have faith, I can move mountains." After hours and hours of shouting and praying, the grasshopper never resurrected, nor were her prayers answered. Subsequently, a downhill journey to unbelief began for her. From simple doubts, it devolved to serious skepticism and finally to total unbelief. She lost

---

[14] "For truly, I say to you, if you have faith as a grain of mustard seed, you will say to this mountain, 'Move from hence to yonder place,' and it will move; and nothing will be impossible to you."

her faith in God, lamenting that He did not answer her prayers. The genesis of her problem, however, was a misguided notion of prayer and of faith. Jesus' word about the faith that moves mountain shouldn't be understood literarily, but metaphorically. The mountain symbolizes obstacles to our faith journey.

How many times do people do weird things and blame God for it? How many times do we expect the Faith to be at the service of our imagination, our whims, and our caprices when it should be the other way around? How many times do we construct for ourselves a god of our own hands and prefer it—even if we do not outright worship it? This is one of the main sources of doubt.

Let me tell another story from the northern part of Nigeria during those boom days of Christian revival in West Africa. A zealous young pastor of an Evangelical church, reveling in the new experience of divine elation, bragged that his faith was comparable to Daniel's in the lion's den. According to the story, he took some members of his church to the zoo and boasted that he could climb the wire fence and not be devoured by the ravenous lions in the zoo. In a blind gesture of pride, he climbed over the fence. A hungry lion crouched at a distance and paused, fixing his eye on his prey, the pitiable pastor. The defiant pastor took the lion's pause as a sign of victory. He turned to the onlookers and was cheered by them—the miracle of the Daniel story came alive! No sooner had their cheers died down than the lion pounced on the pastor and devoured him.

History abounds with people who have done stupid and awful things in the name of faith, as individuals and as groups. Whether it is asking God for a sign about something He's not likely to reveal—such as demanding a revelation about which soccer team or which political candidate will win (this is rampant in Africa, with self-described prophets competing against one another) — or setting a timeline for God to answer a particular prayer intention and then feeling disappointment and doubt when He seems not to come through, we set ourselves up for failure when we try to conform God to our own wants. Often, doubt raises its ugly head when *faith is misapplied because it is misunderstood.* Before we go into the nitty-gritty of this chapter, it is paramount that we state what Christian faith is not.

Christian faith is not magic. It is not the influencing or manipulation of nature by an individual or "cosmic force." For sure, the life of faith is transforming and, when necessary, God can bring messages and miracles to substantiate His presence. But the beneficiary does not determine this; His interventions are by grace, not by merit, for no one *merits* the miraculous.

Christian faith is not pragmatism. It is not about prayers that must produce physical results on demand. It is not a system of predictable inputs and outputs. Yes, if we have faith we can move mountains — namely, the obstacles that prevent us from reaching the goals for which God in Christ has designed us. There have been many cases in which the prayers of the faithful have brought about incredible miracles. Thinking of a direct causal relationship between our faith and answered prayers, however, is misguided. Only God determines the ultimate answers to the prayers of the faithful in His ways and in His time — not the individual.

Faith, as the Protestant theologian Paul Tillich correctly noted, is an expression of one's whole personality. It develops along with the individual's personality, and along with its doubts, difficulties, and challenges. Faith does not totally preclude occasional doubt — for instance, when we feel afraid of the consequences of our belief or feel unsure about some doctrine. In fact, doubt can enhance our faith; it can be the occasion for greater faith because overcoming doubts strengthens our resolve, understanding, and trust in God. Pope Francis once said, "The great leaders of the people of God, like Moses, have always left room for doubt. You must leave room for the Lord, not for our certainties; we must be humble. Uncertainty is in every true discernment that is open to finding confirmation in spiritual consolation."[15]

Therefore, let's say two things about doubt in relation to faith. First, we must not think that the feeling of doubt should always be abysmal. Now, I am not talking about what the *Catechism* calls "voluntary doubt," which "disregards or refuses to hold as true what God has revealed and the Church proposes for belief"; nor am I referring to involuntary doubt that results in "hesitation in believing, difficulty in overcoming objections connected with the faith, or also anxiety aroused by its obscurity." This type of involuntary doubt can be cultivated deliberately. These forms of doubt are dangerous and could lead to "spiritual blindness" (CCC 2088). We have to be careful not to fall into this snare of the enemy.

The more benign doubt to which I am referring is the natural uncertainty resulting from our limitations as people in need of divine grace and light. It emanates from the gray areas of our faith journey. Faith may even start with this form of doubt. It may, in fact, sometimes be rewarding because *a truly sincere doubt due to human limitations will eventually lead to God as the answer.*

The second point about doubt is that it is dangerous if it is initiated voluntarily and if it does not evolve from a heart that is

---

[15] David Gibson, "Excerpts from Pope Francis' Explosive New Interview," *U.S. Catholic,* http://www.uscatholic.org/.

sincere, humble, and open to the truth. When doubt originates from pride and the ego, it is likely to become one of the most terrible of all vices. This is the form of doubt that excludes any unpalatable truth. It assumes that the individual is the sole judge of life and destiny. The individual ensnared by this kind of doubt will not accept, and is not humble enough to acknowledge, that life is bigger than mere logic—bigger than whatever he could ever simply perceive it to be. This form of doubt is the genesis of modern atheism. Its sisters are relativism, which paradoxically assumes that objective reality is doubtful, but subjective reality is certain; and, liberalism, which reduces moral truths to the scale of individual preferences.

Doubt is uncertainty about the truth. At its best, it can encourage us onward to find the truth. But it can also lead to indifference—what philosophers call agnosticism—or worse, to total disbelief—skepticism and atheism.

From Doubt to Faith

There is a sense, as we have said, in which doubt is a prelude to faith. To be tempted to doubt is human. It is also part of human nature to see things from the natural light of reason. Reason, although a spiritual faculty, gathers data from what the senses perceive. This creates a vulnerability to doubt, especially when there is a conflict between apparent material reality and our spiritual calling.

It is human to doubt because we perceive the world from a limited perspective. One of the things I had to explain over and over again when I came to the United States was that Africa is not one people with one common culture, language, and religion. During one holiday, a lady who heard I was traveling to Nigeria to visit my family asked me to say hi to her friend who lives in Kenya. Nigeria and Kenya are four thousand miles apart! How limited our knowledge can be!

In spite of our limited knowledge, objective truth remains. In matters of truth, then, intellectual humility is required. Any person is free to doubt. It is part of the journey of faith. But doubt will be positive when you recognize the need for help and that you perceive things about God, as St. Paul said, "as in a mirror dimly" (1 Cor. 13:12).

In this sense, faith may well increase amid doubts. Doubts show how badly we are in need of divine intervention; we have to be courageous enough to recognize we need help. The ultimate lesson of doubt is the ultimate need of humans for divine help. It reminds us that faith offers what human limitations cannot give. The faith journey is human doubt rescued and transformed. Not to doubt, in fact, is to be divine.

As unaided human reason doubts what it cannot experience or prove with its limited judgment, it needs supernatural help. God shows at our moments of doubt that He is the One who complements our intellects. Human knowledge is complete only when it is linked to the supernatural. Hence, to overcome doubt is to be on the path of faith, constantly connected to God.

Now let us consider the lives of three great biblical figures: Zechariah, John the Baptist, and Thomas the Apostle. In each of these cases, we find various levels of doubt on the one hand and the answers to doubt on the other.

Zechariah's Form of Doubt

Zechariah's form of doubt occurs when we think of God from inside the box of human limitations. It is when we look at God and judge what God can do based on what we know of the laws of nature alone.

In the first chapter of Luke we read that Zechariah and his wife, Elizabeth, were a very godly couple. "They were both righteous before God, walking in all the commandments and ordinances of the Lord blamelessly" (Luke 1:6). Recall that Zechariah was the high priest that year, but even so, he had doubts. He could not come to terms with the fact that God can do what He wants in a manner beyond human comprehension. He had been praying about having children, but it appears he had not fathomed the possibility of a divine answer to his prayers — certainly not by overriding the laws of nature concerning his wife's conception when she was past childbearing age. Thus, when the angel finished delivering the prophecy about the birth of John the Baptist, Zechariah asked the angel, "How shall I know this? For I am an old man, and my wife is advanced in years" (Luke 1:18).

Zechariah's question seems similar to those of Abraham (Gen. 15:8) and Mary (Luke 1:34), but it isn't. Abraham's and Mary's questions sought for hopeful clarifications, whereas Zechariah responded with a spirit of unbelief. His faith was weak, and the only answer from God was dumbness — the high priest was struck mute, unable to announce the goodness of the Lord in the land of the living. Dumbness, therefore, became divine discipline to lead Zechariah to deeper faith. His doubt had been so transformed that when John was born, he testified to what he had seen when he wrote, "His name is John" (Luke 1:63). Then he spoke, bearing witness to the deeds of the Lord among his people.

We find this form of doubt among many. It's easy to have a mold into which we feel God must fit. We think we have it all figured out. If God does not fit into that mold, then we doubt His power. How many times do we limit ourselves by thinking that God can do one thing and not the other simply because it appears unrealistic to us? We forget that God is far beyond human imagination.

Like Zechariah, those with this form of doubt tend to have cold feet in announcing the goodness of the Lord in their daily lives. They seem not to know that God is at work in every breath we take and at each moment of our lives. They are clueless to the realities of divine visitations. Nonetheless, God does not leave them alone. He sends His Spirit to draw them out of unbelief so as to announce His goodness.

John the Baptist's Struggle with Doubt

It might be surprising to hear that John the Baptist, whom the Lord described as the greatest man "among those born of women" (Matt. 11:11), also had his moment of doubt. His type of doubt was the result of a feeling of divine disappointment.

While in prison, John sent his disciples to ask Jesus if He was the One who was to come (Matt. 11:2–3). John may well have doubted if Jesus was really the Messiah. Why? In his humanness — and John was human — he may have hoped and expected that the one about whom he had preached would save him from the hands of Herod. And if Jesus did not do so, who knew if He really was the Christ?

Sometimes we have doubts about our faith in God and the Church because we expect a dramatic positive turn of events in our lives and in society — and then it does not happen. Sometimes, like John in prison, we pray amid pains, sufferings, poverty, joblessness, and injustice. We desperately want Jesus to rescue us, but He seems not to care. At other times, it seems to us that the answers to our prayers have been unnecessarily delayed and we assume that, if God is alive, He should have intervened earlier. The faith journey is often precarious as we meander through the wilderness of uncertainties.

Once a woman who had served the Lord all her life was maligned simply because she spoke the truth about an injustice perpetuated in her community. Her people didn't like her speaking up and chose to make life unbearable for her. She was isolated. At some point, she began to question herself for having spoken a truth that saved the life of a poor, minority child from people who disliked him. The worst of her pain came from those who went to the same church as she did. Her pastor didn't seem to care about her isolation. Doubts began to arise: She questioned why she should fellowship with those people anymore—some of whom had caused her pains. It wasn't the cruelty of the unbelievers that caused her pain, but the cruelty of some of her friends and fellow believers. Her hurt was deep; her struggle with doubt took several sessions of spiritual direction to overcome.

Often, when we have grievances against the members of our worshipping community, we are tempted to transfer our grievances to the Church and to God. Don't we face challenges like the woman described above? It could be a dark time in our family, when unexpected death knocks at our door. The desolation is sometimes protracted, causing us many doubtful moments that can be excruciating. What spiritual writers call "dark night" experiences—of the senses and of the spirit, when the presence of God feels far away—are often felt, by those who are unfamiliar with the interior life, as serious doubts rather than a common experience during the journey of faith.

When things like these happen in our lives, Jesus' response is crucial for us to recall: "Go and tell John what you hear and see: The blind receive their sight and the lame walk, lepers are cleansed and the deaf hear, and the dead are raised up, and the poor have good news preached to them. And blessed is he who takes no offense at me" (Matt. 11:4–6). This means that when we experience doubt about the Lord or about an aspect of our Faith, we should recall what the Lord has done before — the richness of God's glory among us and in the Church — and this will keep us on track. In a more personal way, we can recall the times past when it seemed as if God were not listening, but afterward we realized that He did not abandon us. Simply remember.

The book of Revelation refers to "the word of their testimony" as a tool for overcoming the enemy of faith (Rev. 12:11). In moments of doubt, recount all the blessings, graces, and miracles the Lord has done in your life, in the lives of many, and in the Church. This will keep you from losing your faith.

This tactic is a motivational principle too. It is not simply about positive thinking, but about God-thinking. Think God. Think of God's love and grace. Think of God's everlasting love and goodness — remember those moments in the past when you thought there was no hope and then hope came. Such appeals and remembrances of the blessings of the past help to overcome doubt.

As the Lord reminded John the Baptist, He was equipping him with this tool so he could hold on to what he had already believed. In other words, Jesus' response encouraged John to finish the race and wear the crown of martyrdom, convinced that the Messiah had come not necessarily to save the mortal body from imminent death but to lead us to life eternal. John's possible struggle with doubt ushered in courage amid trials and tribulations. When we overcome this form of doubt, we become stronger, and if we persevere, with the help of the Holy Spirit, we shall become strong enough to stand the greatest test of faith — martyrdom.

Our Journey to God

Thomas's Form of Doubt

Thomas's brand of doubt is the most well known in the New Testament. It is the type of doubt that demands material proof as a precondition of faith. This form applies to all demands for an empirical explanation for spiritual reality. It is most common among people who are very methodical in their thinking and, of course, those who find it hard to accept anything as true that cannot be seen or touched or measured.

In the chapter on providence, I will show how God must not and cannot be explained in the laboratory. Life is deeper than our empirical verification of it. Christian faith, in providing us assurances of the beautiful, the true, and the good, offers a better alternative to the inner yearning of the human person than mere empirical proofs.

Thomas should not have needed to see and touch the side and hands of Jesus, but he wanted it as the only way to believe. The very nature of faith is contradicted if physical proof is its only evidence. In our lives as believers, we had better allow God to be in charge. Sometimes God may use things that are empirical in nature to show us divine wonders and love, but at other times God may simply do otherwise. He is not bound by our expectations!

Our Lord Jesus Christ would not fall for the temptation to use physical evidence as proof of His divinity. The thief on His left as He hung on the Cross wanted Him to perform a miracle by coming down from the Cross so he could believe. The Savior ignored him. Nevertheless, to the thief on His right, who did not look for physical evidence and who simply believed in Jesus' love and innocence, Jesus gave the first testament of heaven's citizenship: "Today, you will be with me in paradise" (Luke 23:43).

Faith and Doubt

Hence, the answer to Thomas's form of doubt are the wounds of the Messiah and the Cross. When the Lord spoke to Thomas, He was not so much giving Thomas proof but announcing a warning. Thus came the confession of all time from the doubter himself: "My Lord and my God!" (John 20:28). This was the very first time Jesus was definitively called Lord by any of His disciples. We must remember that the Lord's response to this type of doubt was a lesson, "Blessed are those who have not seen and yet believe" (John 20:29). It is always a blessing to have faith in God rather than to doubt.

Jesus Understands Your Doubt

Whatever temptations to doubt we face, we have to recognize that our Savior, Jesus Christ, bore all our doubts with us. At the very end of His life, when the journey of our salvation was almost complete, Jesus experienced the most despicable of human injustice and suffering. He cried: "My Lord, my Lord, why has thou forsaken me?" (Matt. 27:46). At that very moment, by that singular act, Jesus, the God-man expressed Himself as many of us do when suffering tests our faith. The cry was in identification with all human sufferings and doubts. It was in solidarity with the "dark night" experiences felt by the faithful all through history. It was a grace-filled cry for the person who needs grace to continue trusting, hoping against all hope, believing against all odds.

On the other hand, Jesus' cry on the Cross is also in identification with the atheist who says there is no God because there are human sufferings. It relates to the South Sudanese who passes through sleepless nights in fear of insecurity and hunger. It identifies with the widow, the orphan, the single mother, the homeless, and all those who have suffered and had cause to doubt God's existence and providence.

Although doubt is part of the human experience, there is an answer to it: We find it in the very words of Jesus in response to the Father in the Garden of Gethsemane, "Not my will, but thine, be done" (Luke 22:42). Whatever happens, let us hold our breath and say with conviction, "God, Your will be done." We may not know what it all means, but we do hold on to God, whose will is supreme and good. That is when doubt is turned on its head and helps us to a lively faith.

Chapter 5

∞

Faith in Relation to Hope and Charity

There is a legendary account of a mother and her three beautiful daughters who suffered martyrdom during the reign of Emperor Hadrian. It was claimed that the mother, the Roman matron Sophia (Wisdom), and her three daughters, Pistis, Elpis, and Agape (Faith, Hope, and Charity), underwent martyrdom for the sake of their Christian faith and were interred on the Aurelian Way. Although we don't know much beyond scanty pieces of information alleged to be about them, I am inspired by their names to think about how the grace of martyrdom flows from faith, hope, and charity. In this chapter we will consider the connection between faith, hope, and charity in our Christian journey.

St. Paul, in his first letter to the Corinthians, describes the gradations of these virtues and concludes by emphasizing that love is the greatest of them all: "So faith, hope, love abide, these three; but the greatest of these is love" (1 Cor. 13:13). The blessed apostle gave several examples clarifying that faith without charity is nonsalvific, but he did not explicitly talk about the connection among the three virtues. That will be our project here, in order to help us to appreciate that Christian faith and spirituality is based on the mystery of the Incarnation and connects us with one another.

Christian faith is incarnate faith. There is no faith in the abstract; rather, every person is called to participate in the mystery of the Incarnation and to live it out daily. It takes two to have faith: God and a human being. It takes two to have Christian faith: Jesus Christ and the Christian. Jesus is our hope, our salvation.

An incarnate faith is grounded in the mystery of the Incarnation — that in the fullness of time God became man in order to save us (Gal. 4:4). Jesus revealed to us the divinity of God, making it possible for us to enter into a profound relationship with Him. Jesus' incarnate nature builds us up not only as individuals but also as a community — the *Mystici Corporis*, "the Mystical Body of Christ" — making it authentically and distinctly Christian.

Christian faith does not work in isolation. Christian faith means identification with and incorporation into Jesus Christ. In addition to the choice of accepting Jesus as our Lord and Savior, we become Christians when we are incorporated into Christ and His Body, the Church, through baptism, which is rightly called the first sacrament of initiation. In this sacrament we are brought into Trinitarian belonging as Christ commanded His apostles to baptize "in the name of the Father and of the Son and of the Holy Spirit" (Matt. 28:19). Through this incorporation, what is personal becomes ecclesial.

Christian faith is personal because it is the individual who makes a personal commitment to be a disciple of Jesus. As Pope Benedict XVI put it, "The act of faith is an eminently personal act that takes place in the most intimate depths of our being and signals a change in direction, a personal conversion. It is *my life* that is marked by a turning point and receives a new orientation." Continuing, the pope states, "My belief is not the result of my own personal reflection, nor the product of my own thoughts. Rather, it is the fruit of a relationship, of a dialogue that involves listening, receiving and a response."[16] The personal aspect of the Christian faith relates to its subjective dimension.

But the Faith is also ecclesial. To paraphrase Pope Benedict again: Every Sunday, we individually recite the Creed as the summary of "*our* Faith," not just *my* Faith. It is therefore the Faith of the community of believers. All through the early Church, as recorded in the Acts of the Apostles, those who accepted Jesus in their lives also became members of *the way* through baptism. They were faithful to the teaching of the apostles and fellowshipped together, united in the breaking of bread and also in the life of prayer (Acts 2:41–42).

Consider the progression of the lives of the early Christians as illustrated above: There is the personal acceptance of the Word, the Trinitarian baptism, then apostolicity, communion (Eucharist), and prayer. In other words, the believers lived a sacramental life, which by its very nature is ecclesial. Thus, Christian faith is not *my* exclusive project or altogether built on a private conversation with Jesus. The claim to be able to "accept Jesus as my personal Lord and Savior" without belonging to the Church under the belief that "no one needs the Church to be saved as a Christian" is theological nonsense and unbiblical. To the contrary, "faith is given to me by God through the community of believers, which is the Church. It numbers me among the multitude of believers in a communion which is not merely sociological but, rather, which is rooted in the eternal love of God, who in

---

[16] Benedict XVI, "On the Ecclesial Nature of Faith," Zenit, October 31, 2012, https://zenit.org/.

himself is the communion of the Father, the Son and the Holy Spirit—who is Trinitarian Love. Our faith is truly personal only if it is also communal. It can be *my* faith only if it lives and moves in the 'we' of the Church, only if it is *our* faith, the common faith of the one Church."[17]

The ecclesial nature of faith is beautifully described in the *Catechism of the Catholic Church*: "'Believing' is an ecclesial act. The Church's faith precedes, engenders, supports and nourishes our faith. The Church is the mother of all believers. 'No one can have God as Father who does not have the Church as Mother' (St. Cyprian, *De unit.* 6: PL 4, 519)" (no. 181).

Christian faith is therefore essentially communal. It neither ignores nor excludes the *ecclesiae*—the Church—whose head is Christ. Individualistic faith isolates itself and thus loses the core ingredient of its Christian identity. This is why true faith is essentially communal. Christian faith connects us with God *and* with each other. It is Christ centered and at the same time charity oriented. It inspires us to love and to relate with others as children of God. Christian faith in action is charity.

Similarly, Christian faith is teleological; it will not find its consummation until it reaches its object, God's Truth,[18] and its ultimate goal, eternal life.[19] This teleological aspect of the Christian faith—that is, the idea that faith is *ordered to* some end or goal—makes it intricately connected with hope. Just as the work of faith is charity, its expectation is in hope.

About the teleological aspect of faith, St. Paul explains that he strives to reach the goal of the Beatific Vision:

[17] Ibid.
[18] Thomas Aquinas, *Summa theologica*, II-II, Q. 1, art. 1.
[19] Benedict XVI, *Spe salvi* 10.

Faith in Relation to Hope and Charity

> Not that I have already obtained this or am already perfect, but I press on to make it my own, because Christ Jesus has made me his own. Brothers, I do not consider that I have made it my own. But one thing I do: forgetting what lies behind and straining forward to what lies ahead I press on toward the goal for the prize of the upward call of God in Christ Jesus. (Phil. 3:12–14)

Faith possesses in a limited form that which is hoped for; it looks up to the final consummation in the life to come. It is like the kingdom of God, which is both now and not yet. The ultimate goal of faith — the Beatific Vision, eternal life — is not to be reached unless faith is sustained to the end. Faith alone, although it originates from God, is not sufficient in itself to reach this goal. But its foundational value is not to be ignored, for without faith, no one can please God (Heb. 11:6), and the righteous is "justified by faith" (Rom. 3:28). How then is it that faith, in itself, is not sufficient to reach the goal of the Beatific Vision?

The answer is found in Scripture, which exposes the communal and teleological dimensions of the Christian faith.

> If I speak in the tongues of men and of angels, but have not love, I am a noisy gong or a clanging cymbal. And if I have prophetic powers, and understand all mysteries and all knowledge, and if I have all faith, so as to remove mountains, but have not love, I am nothing. If I give away all I have, and if I deliver my body to be burned, but have not love, I gain nothing.... When I was a child, I spoke like a child, I thought like a child, I reasoned like a child; when I became a man, I gave up childish ways. For now we see in a mirror dimly, but then face to face. Now I know in part; then I shall understand fully, even as I have been

fully understood. So faith, hope, love abide, these three; but the greatest of these is love. (1 Cor. 13:1–3, 11–13)

Trying to separate faith from the other two theological virtues is like choosing between the lyrics and the music of the Christian journey. James went right to the point: "Faith by itself, if it has no works, is dead" (James 2:17). And St. Thomas Aquinas's teaching that "faith may be without charity, but not as a perfect virtue"[20] expresses the same idea.

When Mother Teresa of Calcutta culminated her faith journey in India, her exceptional acts of love and works of faith on behalf of the people became proofs of her faith. When Charles Lwanga and his companions in Uganda graciously accepted death for their faith by extending a hand of welcome and prayer of forgiveness for their executioners, they were not only confessing their faith, but showing its connection with hope and love.

Think of the Christian missionaries from Poland, Portugal, Ireland, England, Spain, and America, who traveled to different parts of Africa during the most volatile and vulnerable days of evangelization. They were not deterred by mosquito-borne diseases and other dangers. They could not have been motivated by faith alone in exclusion of hope and love. They believed in God; they hoped in the future glory; and therefore they loved unto death.

How Faith Relates to Hope and Charity

What is hope? Our Catholic definition from the *Catechism* is comprehensive:

---

[20] *Summa theologica*, I-II, Q. 65, art. 4.

Faith in Relation to Hope and Charity

Hope is the theological virtue by which we desire the kingdom of heaven and eternal life as our happiness, placing our trust in Christ's promises and relying not on our own strength, but on the help of the grace of the Holy Spirit. (no. 1817)

Pope Benedict XVI's exegesis of Hebrews 11:1 — the classical biblical definition of faith — is relevant here. Hebrews tells us: "Faith is the assurance of things hoped for, the conviction of things not seen." It shows, in unmistakable terms, the nexus between faith and hope. The key insight, as the pope reveals, is in the Greek word *hypostasis*, which is rendered in Latin as *substantia* and here as "assurance." But this isn't the best translation; "substance" is a better English word. The Holy Father stressed this when he wrote:

The concept of "substance" is therefore modified in the sense that through faith, in a tentative way, or as we might say "in embryo" — and thus according to the "substance" — there are already present in us the things that are hoped for: the whole, true life. And precisely because the thing itself is already present, this presence of what is to come also creates certainty: this "thing" which must come is not yet visible in the external world (it does not "appear"), but because of the fact that, as an initial and dynamic reality, we carry it within us, a certain perception of it has even now come into existence.[21]

Correspondingly, Christian faith, like Christian hope, is not faith in *progress*,[22] whose goal is the triumph of reason over reli-

---

[21] *Spe salvi* 2.

[22] Ibid., 18. The idea of faith in progress has its roots in the rationalistic philosophy of Francis Bacon, who wanted to create

gion. Faith in progress is a purely mechanical and materialistic notion of faith that evolved in response to the rise of Marxism and communism. In our age it is intertwined with economic liberalism and the prosperity gospel.

Christian faith is interwoven with hope and love. Hope sustains it, and charity makes it incarnate. Charity is "the theological virtue by which we love God above all things for His own sake, and our neighbor as ourselves for the love of God" (CCC 1822).

St. Thomas Aquinas showed how the three theological virtues are related in the order of precedence and the order of perfection. In the order of precedence, faith comes first, followed by hope and then charity. In Thomas's view, a man loves a thing because he apprehends it as his good. When we believe a person to be good, we develop hope in that person and then proceed to love him or her. But in the order of perfection, charity precedes faith and hope, for it is through charity that they reach their fullness as virtues. Hence, charity is the "mother and the root of all the virtues."[23]

Aquinas's view is grounded in Scripture. St. Paul taught that of all the theological virtues the greatest is love (1 Cor. 13:13). Love, here called charity and understood in this context as Christian love, never fails, because the goal of our faith and what we

---

through rational interpretation a notion of faith that is individualistic and materially oriented. It was later taken up by people such as Juan Bautista Alberdi, and informed the modern theory of evolution. Pope Benedict XVI's *Spe salvi* debunked this heretical interpretation of faith, which may have informed the new-age theology of faith, a faith that is altogether individualistic and, if you will, psychic.

[23] *Summa theologica*, I-II, Q. 62, art. 4.

hope for is the presence of God—and God is Love (1 John 4:8). Thus, although faith and hope can exist without charity, they are not perfect and Christian without charity.

On the other hand, charity is impossible without faith and hope because you have to have faith in God and hope in Him in order to commit your total self in love to Him. As St. Thomas stated:

> Wherefore just as friendship with a person would be impossible, if one disbelieved in, or despaired of, the possibility of their fellowship or familiar colloquy; so too, friendship with God, which is charity, is impossible without faith, so as to believe in this fellowship and colloquy with God, and to hope to attain to this fellowship.[24]

Faith dovetails with hope and matures in charity. The life of faith is truly redemptive if there is hope for a future glory and a true friendship with God, which is charity. The work of Christian faith is charity, and the eternal expectation connected with it is hope. The journey of faith means growing in all three of these essential virtues.

[24] Ibid., Q. 65, art. 5.

Part 2

The Content of Faith

Chapter 6

∞

Belief and Worship

Now we turn to the content of the Christian faith journey — the object of our faith. Believers first profess their belief in God. According to the *Catechism*, "the whole Creed speaks of God, and when it also speaks of man and of the world it does so in relation to God" (no. 199). Let's explore some basic reasons why people of faith make the choices they make and why Christianity is rooted in the belief in one God who revealed Himself as the Father, the Son, and the Holy Spirit.

Human beings by nature are religious. This means we have the natural propensity for truth, and truth includes the supernatural and divinity. We are open to the transcendent and to divine relationship. Religious freedom is built on this fact. The premise of religious freedom is not to facilitate the spreading of false cults; rather, it is the recognition and guarantee of every person's unalienable right to relate with God. The Church is the vanguard of the defense of this freedom for all — Christians and non-Christians — because the Church, and indeed all humanity, has the ultimate responsibility to ask, to seek, to find, and to accept the truth about the ultimate source of being: God. It is simply reasonable to assume that there is only one Ultimate

Being; other claimants to this *ultimacy* are not, by definition, ultimate.

In our generation, just as in many generations before us, people have tried to identify the supernatural objects of belief — the ultimate concern of our existence. For instance, my grandfather was a follower of the polytheistic African Traditional Religion.[25] One of the gods worshipped in the African Traditional Religion of the Igbo clan is Ala, an earth goddess said to be responsible for fertility, rain, and harvest; this is similar to Asherah, the ancient Canaanite goddess of fertility and the seasons, worshipped by Jezebel and her cohorts during the time of Elijah. But before his death, my grandfather hinted to his sons that he had a feeling that a multiplicity of gods is not as safe as one God. He advised his sons to belong to a monotheistic religion, a religion that reduces the tension and uncertainty of having to appease so many gods or goddesses. "Multiplicity of gods," he assessed, "doesn't seem right." This was the way he explained his struggle with the notion of polytheism. His explanation, although pragmatic in character, has some deep insight and appeals to common sense. His was reason in action. The good news: His sons heeded his advice and became Christians.

To be sure, there are other objects of belief that people feel can serve as the "ultimate concern" in their lives. They include humanism, which enthrones man over God; the cult of nationalism, when the state or "the people" is made the object of ultimate

---

[25] Some scholars of African Traditional Religion claim that it is not strictly polytheistic because in some cultures, such as in Igboland, a distinction is made between Chukwu — the most high God — and lesser gods. This, however, is not a common feature in other parts of Africa.

concern; the religion of law, in which the civil law and "order" become values over all else; and hedonism, when pleasure becomes the be-all and end-all of human existence. Although these are not ordinarily considered religions, when they become or demand man's ultimate allegiance, they have become adorned with the status of the supernatural. They become idolatrous cults.

In his revealing and shocking article "Elvis Alive? The Ideology of American Consumerism," the anthropologist Peter Stromberg writes about how consumerism has become a cult and a religion:

> The central sacrament of consumerism is purchase, its daily ritual is entertainment, and its scripture is advertising.... Celebrities are deities because they are the most significant mediators in the consumerist society; they are at once human and God.[26]

This article sheds light on the idolatry of materialistic consumerism. It paints a clear picture of a society in which many attempt, to their own dismay, to replace God with a god of their own creation—or, more precisely, consumption. Herein again lies the fact of our religious nature: Rejection of the true object of worship leads to an improvised form of deity. Try as we may, we cannot run away from having an ultimate allegiance.

But let us get back to the topic at hand: In relation to the obedience of faith, who is God to us? God is the One to whom belongs our ultimate allegiance and love; He is the supreme object of our faith and worship.

---

[26] Peter Stromberg, "Elvis Alive? The Ideology of American Consumerism," *Journal of Popular Culture* 24, no. 3 (Winter 1990): 11–19.

Our Journey to God

Let us briefly consider nine qualities of the God we worship: He is one, holy, just, almighty, the source of truth, a being of revelation and miracles Who is supreme and is love itself.

God Is One

The God in which we believe must be one — that is, one in nature, substance, and essence. There can never be two ultimate beings; otherwise, they are not ultimate. Being the ultimate presupposes not having an equal rival.

We do not accept that there are two ultimate principles, good and evil, as the Manicheans[27] believed. As St. Augustine argued, evil is not being, but a privation of being; we are at our most *alive* when we are good. The true God is indivisible, eternal, unchangeable, and indeed the fullness of being itself: perfection. Belief in a multiplicity of gods contradicts the very idea of a Supreme Being. Besides the one true God, there is no other god. "Hear, O Israel: the LORD our God is one LORD; and you shall love the LORD your God with all your heart, and with all your soul, and with all your might" (Deut. 6:4–5).

God Is Holy

The God Whom we worship must be the Holy One; otherwise we would have no reason to adore Him or regard Him as good. If God were to be equal in status with humans or human institutions,

---

[27] The Manicheans were a heretical group in the time of the early Church who held that evil and goodness were equal opposing forces in the universe. Before his baptism St. Augustine was briefly taken with them.

then looking for answers of an ultimate nature would be a farce. To be truly God, the being of my ultimate concern must be set apart from other contestants for that concern and from the experiential world.

By the same token, this God must be free of all alteration, impurity, and moral decadence. The holy must be uniquely set apart from rivals. We read in Scripture:

Who is like you, O LORD, among the gods? Who is like you, majestic in holiness, terrible in glorious deeds, doing wonders? (Exod. 15:11)

There is none holy like the LORD, there is none besides thee; there is no rock like our God. (1 Sam. 2:2)

There is none like you among the gods, O LORD, nor are there any works like thine. All the nations thou hast made shall come and bow down before thee, O LORD, and shall glorify thy name. For thou art great and doest wondrous things, thou alone art God. (Ps. 86:8–10; see also Ps. 99:1–3; Isa. 40:25; 57:15)

Thus, holiness for God goes beyond being an attribute to being who God is. It predicates other divine attributes: God's love is holy; God's justice is holy; God's mercy is holy; God's power is holy; God's word is holy; and God's commands are holy. All God does is holy.

God Is Just

The God in whom we believe must be just; otherwise He would not be God. The Old Testament word for "just" literally means "straight," and the New Testament word means "equal." To say that God is just means that His ways, actions, and words are straight and right. He is neither duplicitous nor prejudiced, as we are. Scripture uses the words *just* and *righteous* interchangeably. God's justice, which is also His righteousness, flows from His holiness. He treats His creatures as a just judge who shows no partiality. It's like a thread running through the entire plan of God, from creation to redemption: God's ways are straight and right.

This also means that God cannot be controlled by the magical incantations of creatures to show favoritism such as in some indigenous religions, in which it is claimed that their gods can be controlled to do the wish of the people. The justice of the true God can never be altered by human manipulation. Magic or superstition has no place in the plan of the true God.

God Is Almighty

God is almighty. This means that He has absolute power and authority and does whatever He pleases. The key word here is *absolute*. God's power and authority are unlimited. The God worthy of belief must have supreme power over all else and must be answerable to no one. We will consider this attribute of God further in the next chapter.

God Is Truth

The God Who commands our ultimate worship and faith must be One who is not only true but whose very being must be truth itself. His words, commands, and actions—indeed His entire revelation of Himself—must be not just truthful, but the font of truth. This is why the believer can "abandon [himself] in full trust to the truth and faithfulness of his word in all things" (CCC 215).

This attribute is related to God's justness. In the just God there is no lie; all is unchanging truth. The truth does not change with times and circumstances; rather, truth holds all things in order. The God to believe in, the God of truth, holds the entire universe under the umbrella of His absolute order because what He says and what He does emanate from the truth that God *is*. God's actions are a synergy of one word and one will; there is never confusion or ambiguity. This attribute of God assures believers of continuity in their relationship with Him.

God Reveals Himself

The one and only true God must be able to reveal Himself to us, His creatures; otherwise, we could never understand who He is. This is common sense: How could we know the Supreme Being, who is beyond all human reckoning, unless He reveals Himself to us, unveiling His nature? If God were a material being, we would not need any revelation, for we would see Him as we see other things of nature. But insofar as God is pure existence (borrowing a phrase from St. Thomas Aquinas)—beyond matter, indeed the source of existence itself—then the true God must therefore be the God of revelation.

Revelation here is not to be measured by some daydreaming experiences or subjective visions authenticated only by the individual or his close friends. Revelation in this context means that God must have been announced and unveiled, manifested not only to an individual here or there but also to people across the world who would validate that revelation; otherwise He would not be a *universal* God.

Our Journey to God

God Performs Miracles

It follows logically from His all-powerful nature that the true God must have the ability and authority to perform miracles. *Miracle* here is understood as the power to alter the natural course of things — to do things that by the apparent laws of nature are impossible. But with God "all things are possible" (Matt. 19:26). Additionally, this means the ability to set the laws of nature in motion such that miracles become, as it were, natural — even if impossible for us to explain using normal methods.

A God worthy of worship does not need to consult any higher power to perform miracles, nor do these miracles require some strange incantation or magical ritual on our or anyone else's part. God wields the power Himself. When Jesus told the dead to rise, He spoke the word and His word gave life to the dead. When Jesus spoke to the storms, they obeyed him too, because he is God. Any claimant to divine supremacy must have this power.

God Is Supreme

The true God must be supreme above every power, human or angelic. He must be supreme above every institution, religious or political, in order for Him to command our ultimate reverence. He is not and must not be answerable to anyone. Neither can He be limited in the execution of His will. He must possess in Himself all the resources to lead His creation from beginning to end, as well as to orchestrate the *telos* — the purpose or end — of all creatures.

Our God does not need a high priest to compel Him to act. He does not compete for relevance as do the tribal gods of many indigenous religions. A God worthy of worship does not have rivals.

Belief and Worship

God Is Love Itself

"God is love" (1 John 4:8). For this to be true, His love must be gratuitous, boundless, faithful, and everlasting—gratuitous because His creatures can never merit the notice of such a perfect being, boundless because there is no limit to His power, faithful because He is unchanging, and everlasting because He is eternal.

∞

These criteria do not in any way exhaust who God is, nor do they completely explain His being, which is beyond human words. There are many other attributes that describe the living God; all we can do is attempt to use our limited vocabularies to get as close as we can.

If our ultimate concern is something that does not include all these attributes, it is not worthy of the place we have given it. Get your checklist: Is your god one, holy, and just? Is he the almighty and the source of all truth? Has he revealed himself to the world so that he may be known? Does your object of worship have the power to perform miracles? Is he supreme above all else, and is he love itself? If any, some, or all of your answers are not in the affirmative, then your faith in that being or thing is an idolatrous faith—the elevation of finite realities to the rank of Supreme Being.

The question of which being to accept as ultimate was settled thousands of years ago, but some people today reinvent the old controversy and claim it as new. It was settled on Mount Carmel, when the prophet Elijah proposed to the hundreds of prophets of Baal that the God who answered by fire is God indeed (1 Kings 18:24).

The God to believe, therefore, is the One who is this ultimate being before whom and after whom there is no other. God revealed His name to the chosen people, Israel, by making His name known to them because His is the God of revelation. He was preannounced beyond that land, however, so that when He was born in Bethlehem, wise men from the east came to pay Him homage. More important, in the Old Testament, God revealed His name so we may call Him by name, no matter how impossible it is to apprehend Him fully.

> God has a name; he is not an anonymous or coincidental force. To disclose one's name is to make oneself known to others; in a way it is to hand oneself over by becoming accessible, capable of being known more intimately and addressed personally. (CCC 203)

The Church teaches that "God revealed Himself progressively and under different names to His people, but the revelation that proved to be the fundamental one for both the Old and the New Covenants was the revelation of the divine name to Moses in the theophany of the burning bush, on the threshold of the Exodus and of the covenant on Sinai" when God said "I Am who I Am" (CCC 204, 206). As the Nicene-Constantinople council declares "God is unique; there is only one God."[28] He is the Living God.

The consequences of believing in the true God and loving Him with all our heart, strength, and mind are enormous and radically beneficial. As the *Catechism* shows, it means that we shall worship God alone:

> It means living in thanksgiving: if God is the only One, everything we are and have comes from him, "What have

---

[28] *Roman Catechism* I, 2, 2.

you that you did not receive?" (1 Cor. 4:7). "What shall I render to the LORD for all his bounty to me?" (Ps. 116:12).

It means knowing the unity and true dignity of all men: Everyone is made in the image and likeness of God (Gen. 1:26).

It means making good use of created things: faith in God, the only God, leads us to use everything that is not God only insofar as it brings us closer to him, and to detach ourselves from it insofar as it turns us away from him. . . .

It means trusting God in every circumstance, even in adversity. (CCC 224–227)

The object of true faith must be the true God. The chapters that follow elaborate on how God is the God toward whom the Christian faith journey is ordered.

Chapter 7

∞

Our God Is Almighty

The Bible is full of stories of God's power and authority. As a refresher, let's recount a few of the stories—two from the Old Testament and two from the New Testament.

Let's begin in the historical literature of the Old Testament. God promised Abraham and Sarah they would have a son through whose offspring the world would be blessed. From the purely human point of view, the promise was unusual and unrealistic. Abraham and Sarah were getting on in years. When told she would be the mother of Abraham's child, the child of promise, Sarah laughed, betraying the inner doubts locked inside of her heart, as every woman who has passed the age of childbirth knows it is impossible. In response, God spoke the following words to Abraham, "Why did Sarah laugh, and say, 'Shall I indeed bear a child, now that I am old?' Is anything too hard for the LORD? At the appointed time I will return to you, in the spring, and Sarah shall have a son" (Gen. 18:13–14). Needless to say, Sarah conceived and bore a son as the Lord had promised, underscoring the fact that with God, "all things are possible" (Matt. 19:26).

Then, many generations later, when God rescued the nation of Israel from bondage in Egypt He led them through the wilderness and miraculously provided them manna for food. Nevertheless, the Israelites complained because they could not enjoy the delicacies they were accustomed to eating in Egypt. In response to their grumbling, God promised to give them meat for the entire period. The people were doubtful, as was Moses, who expressed his concerns to God: "The people among whom I am number six hundred thousand on foot; and you have said, 'I will give them meat, that they may eat a whole month!' Shall flocks and herds be slaughtered for them, to suffice them? Or shall all the fish of the sea be gathered together for them, to suffice them?" (Num. 11:21–22).

In response to Moses, God asked another question — a question vitally important to us today — "Is the Lord's hand shortened? Now you shall see whether my word will come true for you or not" (Num. 11:23). Certainly, God's hand is not shortened; nothing limits His power. God miraculously provided quails in the wilderness, as he had promised. God's ability to provide beyond human understanding is a running thread throughout Israel's story. I can't say it enough: our daily faith motto should be "With God All Things Are Possible."

In the New Testament, we have many beautiful stories of God's omnipotence. The sixth chapter of John's Gospel records that when Jesus was teaching the crowd, He observed that His audience was hungry, for they had been with Him for a long time without food. When He looked up and saw a great crowd coming toward Him, He said to Philip, "How are we to buy bread, so that these people may eat?" He asked this only to test Philip, for he already knew what He was going to do. God always sees the finish line from the start.

Philip responded incredulously that half a year's wages "would not buy enough bread for each of them to get a little." Andrew pointed out that a boy had five loaves of bread and two fishes, "but what are they among so many?" But Jesus calmly said, "Make the people sit down." There were about five thousand men, not even counting women and children.

> Jesus then took the loaves, and when he had given thanks, he distributed them to those who were seated; so also the fish, as much as they wanted. And when they had eaten their fill, he told his disciples, "Gather up the fragments left over, that nothing may be lost." So they gathered them up and filled twelve baskets with fragments from the five barley loaves, left by those who had eaten. When the people saw the sign which he had done, they said, "This is indeed the prophet who is to come into the world!" (John 6:11–14)

Wow! What power must one possess to accomplish this kind of miracle — in full view of thousands of people and yet known to only a few.

Moving ahead to John's eleventh chapter we find the story of the Savior visiting His good friend when many thought it was too late. After hearing of Lazarus's illness, Jesus waited for two days before setting out to see him, and it seemed He had waited too long. But He had a plan. God always has a plan — a better plan than any we can devise with our limited reason. So He set out to see Lazarus.

By the time Jesus arrived, four days had gone by since Lazarus had succumbed to his illness. Everyone at the scene was afraid, despairing, or, in the case of those who were suspicious of Jesus, sarcastic. Lazarus was dead, and the game was over. The Apostles were afraid and did not want Jesus to go into Judea because the Jews were looking for Him to kill Him. Martha, who despairingly cried, "Lord, if you had been here, my brother would not have died," had not conceived the possibility of the power of Jesus to raise her brother from the dead. And the Jews who observed Jesus weep said sarcastically, "Could not he who opened the eyes of the blind man have kept this man from dying?" For all these people, the death of Lazarus was final; the dead are dead.

When Jesus asked to be shown where Lazarus was buried and for the stone covering the tomb to be removed, Martha replied, "Lord, by this time there will be an odor, for he has been dead four days." As we know, Jesus performed the miracle and raised Lazarus from death after four days in the tomb. The meaning of His initial wait to come to Lazarus was revealed: in the Jewish understanding, after three days the dead have passed to a place of no return to physical life. At four days after death, Lazarus was considered to be totally beyond this world. But Jesus made the impossible possible with just a sigh and a command. God creates out of nothing. He gives life out of nothing.

These stories are among many in Scripture that demonstrate God's almighty power. Many New Testament accounts also show Jesus Christ to be truly God. From the creation narrative to the eschatological visions in the book of Revelation, we have substantial testimony to the power of God. It is therefore no surprise that of all His attributes, only His almighty power is mentioned in the Apostles' Creed. Almighty power is an attribute that necessarily follows from God's divinity. It expresses the idea of absolute authority over all of creation.

The concept of power has been an object of great discussion among sociologists and political philosophers. In any given situation, the person who has power calls the shots regarding the disposition of material goods, events, and even fellow people. Usually, when a political leader wields power, he or she does so within the framework of the law—civil or natural. Power wielded within the confines of the law is legitimate. Power wielded outside the confines of the law wreaks havoc on society. When a ruler is said to have "absolute" power it really is hyperbole. No human could ever have absolute power.

For God, the case is different since He is almighty and always just. To say that God is almighty entails three main ideas:

- God's power is absolute.
- God's power is universal.
- God's power is eternally integrated.

God's Power Is Absolute

Think about the most powerful people in the world—CEOs, presidents, and so forth. These people wield considerable power in their companies and countries, but still there are always limitations to what they can accomplish. CEOs are limited by boards of directors and their competitors; political leaders are limited by other authorities within the government and, failing that, by the people. Even the most authoritarian leaders in the world must constantly shore up their power against threats.

This also applies to religious leaders. The most powerful religious leader in the world remains the pope, although this power is exercised most perfectly in service. Nevertheless, even the pope kneels and bows before almighty God. He is answerable to Somebody. An old story is told of a pope who went into his private chapel at night, removed his skullcap, and placed it on God's altar, saying, "This is your Church. Take care of it because I need to go to bed. I will help you carry it tomorrow. Good night."

Thus, neither the pope nor the most powerful political leader nor the most powerful CEO has unlimited power. With God, the situation is different. God has absolute power; it is unlimited and complete, neither shared with nor granted by anyone else. God does whatever He wills; He has no need to consult with anyone. He has all it takes to accomplish what He does because He *is existence itself*. Thus, God is also all knowing. The prophecy of Isaiah beautifully expresses this idea: "Whom did he consult for his enlightenment, and who taught him the path of justice, and taught him knowledge and showed him the way of understanding?" (40:14).

God's willing and existence are identical. Hanging on the Cross, Jesus spoke to the thief at His right side: "Today you will be with me in paradise" (Luke 23:43). So it happened that a thief entered heaven just by the very word of Jesus. He has *absolute* power over life and death, over heaven and hell, for all power belongs to Him (Matt. 6:13). God can therefore do all things (Matt. 19:26; Mark 14:36), for nothing is impossible for Him (Luke 1:34–37). God is *absolutely* able to fulfill promises (Rom. 4:21). God is *absolutely* able to save us and to do so forever (Isa. 63:1; Ps. 54:1; Rom. 1:16; Heb. 7:25), to set us free from danger (Dan. 3–4), to protect us (Ps. 79:1; 91:1), and to rescue us (Ps. 79:11).

We, in and of ourselves, may be limited in what we can do to fulfill our purpose in life. But God isn't limited in His ability to accomplish His will in and through us, if we allow Him to lead us. No matter how intelligent we may be, no matter how strategic our plans for the future are, without God nothing worthwhile will happen.

God's Power Is Universal

God's power is absolute because it is universal. This means God is not limited by space and time. After all, God created space and time! In the beginning, it was all chaos. It was God who by the power of His word ordered space and time and the rules by which they function. God is pre-time.

One of the challenges to the Catholic Church in Africa is the residual belief from African Traditional Religion that deities are territorial. African Traditional Religion, like most indigenous or traditional or nature religions, has an idea of deities as gods of specific places, peoples, shrines, or aspects of human life. The god takes charge of those events and lives for a limited time. Thus, the concept of a universal God who has absolute power not limited by territory or time is not readily assimilated by indigenous peoples. From time to time, people who have become Christians fall back to their prior idolatrous notions of God as territorial.

I've seen this in the way some people use the sacramentals of the Church. The Church is rich in symbols, icons, and sacramentals—such as holy water, blessed salt, and so on. We know that religious language is symbolic and in many cases sacramental in nature. Nevertheless, sometimes we observe an abuse of the proper use or meaning of these sacred signs. I have had to explain to some families that the holy water we use is not a magical element that brings about miracles. Crucifixes are not talismans like those used in pagan cults. They are simply sacramental. Their use is to inspire us and help us connect with Almighty God, who has the power to bring about His will, whether in the form of a miracle or a less noticeable pouring out of grace.

Similarly, God's universal power covers my personal life as well as our collective existence as a people. We need to recognize that God has the overriding control over our lives. Although He grants us the freedom to make choices, this freedom does not in any way limit His absolute power over us. God is our ultimate Lord, to whom we pay homage. God is the master of history, governing hearts and events in keeping with the divine will. "It is always in thy power to show great strength, and who can withstand the might of thy arm?" (Wisd. 11:21).

God's Power Is Eternally Integrated

The *Catechism* teaches that God's almighty power is in no way arbitrary: "In God, power, essence, will, intellect, wisdom, and justice are all identical. Nothing therefore can be in God's power which could not be in his just will or his wise intellect (St. Thomas Aquinas, *STh* I, 25, 5, ad. I)." Thus, whatever God does is holy and perfect.

I suspect that some will now ask the age-old questions: If God is all powerful and all wise, then why is there evil in the world? And if God's power is absolute and universal, why should we pray, since God does whatever He wills?

Many great minds have answered these questions, and the arguments never end. Let's begin with some rhetorical questions: If there is no all-powerful God, then why has evil not overtaken goodness, beauty, and truth, despite its insidious and invasive character? If God is not all powerful, how is it that so many men and women still chant the *Deo gratia* amid the menacing ruins of evil? How is it that so many still see evil for what it is and do not mistake it for the good? We speak of evil and see the ugly face of evil in the world because the good God has put in our hearts a seed for goodness.

With respect to our personal free will, God's absolute power implies His absolute honor of the freedom *He chose to bequeath to us* as rational creatures. In His almighty nature, God models for us the right use of power and authority and wants us to fulfill the very goal He had in creating us—namely, to choose from nature's beatitudes the path we want for ourselves. God's absolute power is indeed exercised every day in freedom; we are, in a sense, delegates of that freedom, deputized to live out God's will in freedom here on earth.

We said earlier that by His gratuitous love and consistent with His being, God gave us freedom and equipped us to cooperate with His providence. This means that God wills us to have the privilege and power to change things and situations around us. God endorses the legitimate use of this right, but it is not absolute. It is not legitimate when exercised in isolation from the delegator.

For example, a Catholic bishop of the Latin Rite who is a local ordinary of a diocese cannot remain legitimate if he severs communication—and therefore communion—with the pope. Nor can an ambassador of a nation remain legitimate if he breaks ties with the represented country. We too cannot legitimately use the power of co-creation if we sever ourselves from our Creator. If this connection is severed, there are bound to be consequences—consequences that are never good for us.

In our relationship with God in the faith journey, one of the virtuous habits that keep us focused and properly disposed to His direction is prayerful obedience. Prayer in this sense is basically a communication; it places us where we belong and recognizes the place of God in the dialogue. Prayer becomes the place of encounter between God and us, His delegates. Through prayer, we delegates can tap into and execute some of the qualities of God as the Almighty.

This encounter is perfectly achieved in the Eucharist. The Eucharist is the ultimate prayer: a sacrifice of God, the Son, to the Father and of humanity to God. It is where we can draw from the almighty power of God so that we can make wonderful things happen for the good of believers. It is in the Eucharist that heaven and the attributes of our God in heaven are uniquely instantiated in time, tangibly and before our eyes.

The implications of the theology of the almighty power of God in our lives are huge. First, it inspires us not to live in fear, for the "Lord of Hosts is with us and the God of Jacob is our stronghold" (Ps. 46:11). The faith journey is a courageous ride we take with confidence in divine providence and sovereignty. Faith empowers us. We do not need to fear death, hunger, pestilence, poverty, or whatever else might appear in our way. We are assured of the supremacy of the Lord in our lives: "Little children, you are of God, and have overcome them; for he who is in you is greater than he who is in the world" (1 John 4: 4).

Second, our weaknesses are not a barrier to God's power to save us. Severing ties with God by rejecting His friendship can be a barrier, but it is one that *we* erect. Our God-given freedom can be our only nemesis only if, like the fallen angel, we use it to tell God that we will not serve Him. We have to step away from our weaknesses and hand ourselves over to God's rule. He can transform our weaknesses to strength for the glory of His name.

Third, we should not allow ourselves to be taken in by the devil. Satan and his works and pranks, as expressed in witchcraft and voodoo but also in institutionalized evil and injustice, should not be given free reign. We stave off evil by proclaiming the good news of our very existence; evil, as St. Augustine teaches, degrades existence itself. The devil is not our God; he has no absolute power to do anything. The Lord Jesus Christ has already achieved victory over the devil's tactics, and we equally are victorious in Christ, who is our strength.

If we really understood the power of God, we would not give so much credit to Satan. We would realize that because God is the Creator, Satan is but a creature—a fallen angel. We would know that God's power is infinite, while Satan's power is finite and indeed miniscule. God is not battling with Satan with the hope of defeating him; Satan is already a defeated foe, whose final demise is certain (John 12:31; 16:11; Luke 10:18). In the meantime, God is allowing Satan and his rebellion to achieve His purposes (see 2 Cor. 12:7–10). As Venerable Archbishop Fulton J. Sheen said, "Evil may have its hour, God has his day."[29]

---

[29] Fulton J. Sheen, "Three Times in a Nation's History," in *Life Is Worth Living* (San Francisco: Ignatius Press, 1999).

Chapter 8

The Faithful Father

The Christian faith journey is a life in relationship with the Trinity—the person of the Father and the person of the Son and the person of the Holy Spirit. Our faith in God as Father draws us into a deeper appreciation of the reality of the paternal role of God in our lives. In His love for us, His children, our eternal Father is radically different from earthly fathers, whose love can be inconstant. This chapter will explore how the God in whom we believe is our Father, and how and why His love for His children demonstrates the ideal love of a father.

Let us read from the words of our Lord and Savior Jesus Christ to Mary Magdalene shortly after the Resurrection as He anticipates His ascension to heaven:

> Jesus said to her, "Do not hold me, for I have not yet ascended to the Father; but go to my brethren and say to them, I am ascending to my Father and Your Father, to my God and your God." Mary Magdalene went and said to the disciples, "I have seen the Lord"; and she told them that he had said these things to her. (John 20:17–18)

God, you will notice, is both *the* Father and *our* Father. In the Old Testament, one of the most prominent images of God is that of the Liberator. This idea was born out of the Exodus, when God with powerful and outstretched hand delivered His chosen people from bondage in Egypt in fulfillment of His words to Moses:

> Say therefore to the people of Israel, "I am the LORD, and I will bring you out from under the burdens of the Egyptians, and I will deliver you from their bondage, and I will redeem you with an outstretched arm and with great acts of judgment, and I will take you for my people, and I will be your God; and you shall know that I am the LORD your God, who has brought you out from under the burdens of the Egyptians. And I will bring you into the land which I swore to give to Abraham, to Isaac, and to Jacob; I will give it to you for a possession. I am the LORD." (Exod. 6:6–8)

Thereafter, by God's initiative, He entered into a covenant relationship with Israel that culminated at Mount Sinai (Exod. 24). By this covenant, Israel became "a people holy to the LORD [their] God" (Deut. 26:19). This means that they belonged to God in a special way. A reciprocal relationship was established: "I will be your God and you will be my people" (Lev. 26:12; Jer. 7:23).

God's covenant with His people stipulates that they honor and worship Him, the one and only God. Leading up to the confirmation of the covenant at Mount Sinai, God had emphasized that He is a jealous God who cannot tolerate the worship of other gods and will punish to the third and fourth generation anyone who does not respect His holiness (Exod. 20:5).

The Israelites gradually came to realize that there is no other God but Yahweh. This developed into an awareness that the God who liberated Israel is the same God who created the world. From the Exodus experience of liberation came the Genesis revelation of creation. If God is the Creator of all things and of all people, then God is the God of all.

Similarly, the people of the Old Law understood that this God who is the Liberator and the Creator is the one who is their transcendent Father, supreme above all His creatures but at the same time close to them. They belong to Him as children belong to their father by the fact of the covenant.

Although the image of God as Father is not central in the faith of Israel, it is lived in their experience with Him. The fatherhood of God was not based *primarily* on the idea of God as Creator but on the notion of God as Liberator who entered into a covenant relationship with Israel. We read in Exodus that God called Israel His first-born son: "And you shall say to Pharaoh, 'Thus says the Lord, Israel is my first-born son, and I say to you, "Let my son go that he may serve me"; if you refuse to let him go, behold, I will slay your first-born son'" (Exod. 4:22–23). If Israel is Yahweh's first-born son, then Yahweh is Israel's father.

Further revelations of God's fatherhood are seen in the prophets, which in most cases are more explicitly stated. In the prophecy of Isaiah, God is addressed as Father:

Look down from heaven and see, from thy holy and glorious habitation. Where are thy zeal and thy might? The yearning of thy heart and thy compassion are withheld from me. For thou art our Father, though Abraham does not know us and Israel does not acknowledge us; thou, O LORD, art our Father, our Redeemer from of old is thy name. (Isa. 63:15–16)

This text expresses the idea of the absolute authority of God over Israel and His saving concern and loving tenderness toward His people. It is also a plea for mercy and for God's continued protection. He is Father because He is the origin of everything, and His authority is transcendent — surpassing all human knowledge or imagination.

In the New Testament, God's fatherhood is clearly expressed in a relationship. Jesus revealed that God is Father in an "unheard-of-sense," as many Church documents explained it:

> He is Father not only in being Creator; he is eternally Father in relation to his only Son, who is eternally Son only in relation to his Father: "No one knows the Son except the Father, and no one knows the Father except the Son and any one to whom the Son chooses to reveal him" (Matt. 11:27). (CCC 240)

God is our Father because we share in the sonship of His Son, our Lord Jesus Christ. An ancient Church phrase beautifully describes that we are made "sons in the Son" through baptism. St. Paul's letter to the Romans emphasizes that through the Spirit, we are given the privilege of calling God *Abba*, "Father" (Rom. 8:15).

Saint Ephrem of Syria rightly said that "earthly fathers are called fathers, but He is the true Father.... The terms 'father' and 'son' by which they have been called are borrowed names that through grace have taught us there is a single true Father and that He has a single true Son."[30] If this is the case, it means that the eternal relation of the Father and the Son is not a metaphor.

---

[30] St. Ephrem, Hymn 46 on the Faith.

Instead, as Scott Hahn argues, "human fatherhood is more like a metaphor for God's eternal fatherhood."[31] Scripture attests that it is from God that all fatherhood, earthly or heavenly, derives its name (see Eph. 3:15).

Since this is the case, then our Eternal Father embodies the ideal qualities of fatherhood and makes us his children and thus beneficiaries of those qualities. The best way to describe this is in relationship with the Son, and through the Son to us. One word that summarizes the shades of God's paternal relationship with us is *faithful*—unfailing love profoundly flowing through God's revelation in Christ.

God's Fatherhood Is Unfailing Love

Love is characterized by the nature of the lover. Here's what that means: If the person doing the loving has a human nature, then the love is of a human nature and must therefore have the peculiarities of human nature. But human nature, as we know, has its limitations. It is contingent and conditional. It is prone to expiration, either in death or as we lose interest in the object of love. Finally, human love seeks its special interests or gratification—such, for example, is the love between married couples. When two people decide to marry, they are making a bold statement that they are choosing to exclude others from that special type of love relationship. Married love excludes.

On the other hand, if love is of godly nature, then it must have the capacity of divinity; it is supernatural and unlimited. God's love is unlimited because His nature has no limitations.

---

[31] Scott Hahn, *Understanding "Our Father": Biblical Reflections on the Lord's Prayer* (Steubenville, OH: Emmaus Road, 2002), 10.

His faithful love is beyond that of changeable humans because He is constant and eternal. The love of God is all embracing; it does not pick and choose among its objects. Such is the love of our Eternal Father.

Thus, we have a Father who is eternally faithful. He is unfailing in His love, care, provision, and promises for us, His children. Even when we fail Him, He is ever faithful. He is the one who is patient with us and does not want any of us, His children, to be lost (see 2 Pet. 3:9). He is a father, who will not refuse us anything that He knows will be for our good:

> What father among you, if his son asks for a fish, will instead of a fish give him a serpent; or if he asks for an egg, will give him a scorpion? If you then, who are evil, know how to give good gifts to your children, how much more will the heavenly Father give the Holy Spirit to those who ask him! (Luke 11:11–13)

God is also a father who can never forget His children. We believe God's fatherly love is comparable to that of a mother, who cannot forget her baby: "Can a woman forget her sucking child, that she should have no compassion on the son of her womb? Even these may forget, yet I will not forget you" (Isa. 49:15).

God's Fatherhood Is Both
Personal and Universal

God's fatherhood is personal because He knows each of us — His sons and daughters — by name (Isa. 43:1–2). He cares about our unique situations. God as a Father watches every step we take and is ever ready to show us His love.

The Faithful Father

But God's fatherhood is also universal because, as Jesus taught us to pray, He is "our Father" and not just "my Father." Because God is *our* Father, the Christian faith proposes that there is a filial relationship between Him and all persons. All of us belong to one family, and when incorporated into the Church we become God's family with God as our Father. Thus, God is not a Father only to the Jewish people, or, for that matter, only to Africans or Americans or Europeans. He is not a Father only to the saint but also to the sinner, for He makes His rain fall on the sinner and the just at the same time (Matt. 5:45). He is the Father of all.

Similarly, by the fact of His fatherhood, we belong to one family, the family of God. The Church becomes a home for all of God's children. An ancient hymn reads, "Like olive branches around the table of the lord, so God's children in the Church."

The *Catechism* also reminds us that, although we refer to God's fatherhood,

> God's parental tenderness can also be expressed by the image of motherhood (cf. Isa. 66:13; Ps. 131:2), which emphasizes God's immanence, the intimacy between Creator and creature.... God transcends the human distinction between the sexes. He is neither man nor woman: he is God. He also transcends human fatherhood and motherhood, although he is their origin and standard (cf. Ps. 27:10; Eph. 3:14; Isa. 49:15): no one is father as God is Father. (CCC 239)

The idea of God's motherhood is also expressed in the prophecy of Isaiah: "As one whom his mother comforts, so I will comfort you; you shall be comforted in Jerusalem" (66:13).

Our faith journey leads us into a relationship with God, who is not only our Creator and Liberator but also our faithful, unfailing

Father. Let's conclude with the words of a hymn that has become popular especially in Africa:

> I have a father who never fails.
> I have a father who never fails.
> I have a father who never fails,
> Who never fails,
> Who will never fail
> Forevermore.

Chapter 9

∞

The Provider

I am fond of technology and innovative products. I must confess, however, that I am often clueless about how to use all the latest gadgets. Despite my shortcomings, I have come to learn a good deal about inventors, innovation, and product development—and I have found what I've learned to be relevant in my understanding of divine providence.

Innovators and product developers think in terms of both the short run and the long run. In the short run, they work out the details of the product or service they want to develop; and, in the long run, they consider their product's viability in the competitive marketplace. For example, several years ago IBM held an "Innovation Jam"—a kind of online suggestion forum in which they invited customers and employees worldwide to submit ideas for new products and services. The session generated about 37,000 ideas from 104 countries across the globe. The company's Research and Development Department sorted all these ideas and selected only ten products, businesses, and services they thought were likely to be a hit and that they planned to develop. Ever since, they have been working on manufacturing and advertising these products; it is likely some have already hit the market.

Innovators take their time and painstakingly plan their products and services so that those products and services will be of competitive value to their consumers. There are many stages to this development and management process, from idea generation through focus groups and testing and finally to market.

If simple manmade products go through this complex, intelligent process, how about the making of the entire universe — and in particular human beings? Would you not think that we are intelligently, purposefully made? Don't you think that there is a provider for the enormous world and an intelligent mankind? Of course there is, and we may call the process — the dispositions by which the Maker guides creation toward perfection — divine providence.

There are two broad ways to talk about divine providence; one gets at it implicitly and the other explicitly. The former is from a scientific point of view and the other from a divine point of view. Whichever route we choose to take, it will lead us to one conclusion: There is a divine Provider, and the world is the fruit of His providence. This way of seeing providence is rooted in the faith life.

Scientific Justification of Divine Providence

Since the nineteenth century, some scientists have furthered the theory of scientific evolution. The goal, for some of the proponents, is to give an alternative explanation about the origin of the material world contrary to creation and in justification of the assumption that only the material world is real.

While scientific investigations are commendable and often quite important, it is easy to observe how flawed is the very premise of the explanation of the origin of things based exclusively on scientific evolution. My objection is to the *exclusive* claim made by some evolution proponents that *only* material forces have acted on things through time. I mean here not just Darwinian evolution but the broadly materialist, deterministic view of reality—that everything that exists and takes place is merely the working out of energy and matter with no supernatural component. The first assumption in this view of existence, far from being a scientific claim about the *how* of things, in fact smuggles in bogus, incoherent philosophy about *why* living things exist that cannot be scientifically tested.

The evolutionists who uphold an exclusively materialistic view of the origin of things must assume that at some point "nothing" existed—and then that nothing somehow gave rise to the elements that in time resulted in the physical world.

This is the most unscientific theory in human history. Common sense tells us that without outside intervention nothing can never become something; zero plus zero can never equal one. The strict materialists' claims is deeply unscientific. At best, it is a philosophical opinion cloaked in the mantle of empirical scientific inquiry.

So, using simple scientific reasoning—there must be some intervening variable for nothing to become something. This variable must predate or be distinct from the void in order for it to be able to transform it into something.

It also stands to reason—and this is where science really trips up—that anything that predates "nothingness" is eternal, and eternity is beyond the purview of the science laboratory. If we're going to accept that something (or Someone) had to act to bring something into being (which we must), then we cannot affirm that *only* the scientific method allows us to understand reality. It's a simple contradiction.

Thus, the evidence tells us that the origin of all things is based on something—a being, a principle, a variable, whatever you want to call it—that allowed nothing to become something, and that something continues perfecting to this day. Evolutionary theory may tell us *how* existing things have developed, but it cannot tell us *why* or *how* things came to exist in the first place. This takes us to the more logical and compelling view about the origin of things and of life: the theological explanation. This view makes sense of the evidence all around us in a more comprehensive way.

The Theological Explanation of Divine Providence

We come now to the Genesis story of creation. The inspired authors, through human language, describe how and why things came to be. The central message, no matter how the story is told and interpreted, can be reduced to one simple, logical premise: There was a Creator who created things out of nothing. This explains the missing variable in the materialists' thesis.

The second logical premise is this: Creation was undertaken in wisdom, not as the product of any necessity or blind fate or chance. All existence proceeds from the Maker's free will (CCC 295) as the Scriptures affirm: "Thou didst create all things, and by thy will they existed and were created" (Rev. 4:11). "O LORD, how manifold are thy works! In wisdom hast thou made them all; the earth is full of thy creatures" (Ps. 104:24).

God creates *ex nihilo*, "out of nothing." He is not like the carpenter, who needs the wood to make furniture, or the carmaker, who needs metal, plastic, and fiber to manufacture. God is not like the innovators of the world, who have to brainstorm with their research-and-development teams to figure out the materials needed to transform a concept into a product. God is the only

The Provider

One Who can make something out of nothing; indeed He gives all things their very existence. Whatever God does is done with the greatest care and provision, for God's being is infinitely more than we could ever imagine.

This is the fundamental missing link in any theory of creation and evolution that excludes the reality of providence. Now, how does God create existence from nonexistence since He has no material to rely on? As believers, we know that God creates freely by His word and in His wisdom.

> For he spoke, and it came to be; he commanded, and it stood forth (Ps. 33:9).

> The voice of the LORD is powerful, the voice of the LORD is full of majesty. The voice of the LORD breaks the cedars, the LORD breaks the cedars of Lebanon. He makes Lebanon to skip like a calf, and Sirion like a young wild ox (Ps. 29:4–6).

> All things were made through him, and without him was not anything made that was made. In him was life, and the life was the light of men (John 1:3–4).

Creation, therefore, is not a "necessary emanation from the divine substance" (CCC 296). Rather, God creates freely by His wisdom, and as a result His creation is ordered (CCC 299). If human innovators plan short term and long term before they make a product, and each product is intelligently put together, how could humanity and the rest of natural creation be a product of chance? Why is there a radical disconnect between the constitution of humans and their own creativity? How could human beings, products of chance, become developers of such well-planned products?

You are not a product of chance, and the beautiful world you live in is not an accidental byproduct of time. You cannot look at and admire the wonders of creation and say these are all products of chance. In the recent past, I toured across the west coast of the United States and saw breathtaking sites—from Pismo Beach to Yosemite, from the Grand Canyon to Sequoia Park. One cannot be blind to how perfectly these places are put together.

God created us in wisdom. Pause for a moment and think about the complexity of our anatomy. Reflect on how you developed from a fertilized egg, and how that zygote held all the genetic information needed to create your complete body with nearly forty trillion cells. Furthermore, all that genetic information is found in each and every cell. Consider also the collaboration among your trillions of cells—more than the stars in the visible galaxies—working perfectly in order as orchestrated by an intelligent Maker. The Scripture confirms we are intricately fashioned in our mothers' wombs (Ps. 139:13–16).

God, who has graced us with all this beauty and orderliness, will not allow us to fade for want of care. He provides for us. He has the power to do so since He makes things out of nothing.

> Through the Holy Spirit, [God can] give spiritual life to sinners by creating a pure heart in them, and bodily life to the dead through the Resurrection. God "gives life to the dead and calls into existence the things that do not exist" (Rom. 4:17). And since God was able to make light shine in darkness by his Word, he can also give the light of faith to those who do not yet know him. (CCC 298)

To use modern computer-technology language, God has all the hardware and software needed to maintain our life at its best. And He sees to it that we are taken care of in the way that best serves the ultimate purpose for which we were made—eternal communion with Him.

> God does not abandon his creatures to themselves. He not only gives them being and existence, but also, and at every moment, upholds and sustains them in being, enables them to act and brings them to their final end. (CCC 301)

For this reason we are encouraged not to be preoccupied with our daily living: "Therefore do not be anxious about tomorrow, for tomorrow will be anxious for itself. Let the day's own trouble be sufficient for the day" (Matt. 6:34). Be not afraid. He who made us has plans for our lives and our future. Although the earth should rock, societies change, neighbors disrupt our lives, and the future appear bleak, God is our Faithful Provider. Even though political authorities disappoint, economies crumble, and the world brings evil and depressing news, the Lord is still God and will lead His creation to its end. Let this blessed assurance give us confidence: The Lord is with us; He is our provider and our salvation. He will lead us to the goal for which we were set at the beginning of time. And faith in Him will see us through.

Our faith journey rests in the provident God, who sees to it that we are sustained and have all we need to reach our eternal goal. By so doing we are graced to be the disciples of His providence.

Chapter 10

∞

Disciples of Divine Providence

In the previous chapter we talked about how God is our ultimate provider. Let's now make one more crucial point about creation with respect to divine providence. It is ancient Catholic teaching that "the universe was created 'in a state of journeying' (*in statu viae*) toward an ultimate perfection yet to be attained, to which God has destined it. We call 'divine providence' the dispositions by which God guides his creation toward this perfection" (CCC 302). In order for this to happen, God, out of His gratuitous love, involves *us* as free responsible agents of His providence.

God is not a micromanager. He is not a boss who gives a precise job description and does not allow the employees to use their initiative to execute it. God delegates and allows us to make our own choices about how our lives will reflect His will. He gives us the gift of freedom so that we will be able to work for the perfection of His plan and purpose for our lives and others'. St. Augustine once said that the "God who created you without you will not save you without you." Here's the *Catechism*:

> God is the sovereign master of his plan. But to carry
> it out he also makes use of his creatures' co-operation.

This use is not a sign of weakness, but rather a token of almighty God's greatness and goodness. For God grants his creatures not only their existence, but also the dignity of acting on their own, of being causes and principles for each other, and thus of co-operating in the accomplishment of his plan. (CCC 306)

In the book of Genesis we hear this divine mandate beautifully and categorically spelled out for us:

Then God said, "Let us make man in our image, after our likeness; and let them have dominion over the fish of the sea, and over the birds of the air, and over the cattle, and over all the earth, and over every creeping thing that creeps upon the earth. So God created man in his own image, in the image of God he created him; male and female he created them. And God blessed them, and God said to them, "Be fruitful and multiply, and fill the earth and subdue it; and have dominion over the fish of the sea and over the birds of the air and over every living thing that moves upon the earth." And God said, "Behold I have given you every plant yielding seed which is upon the face of all the earth, and every tree with seed in its fruit; you shall have them for food. And to every beast of the earth, and to every bird of the air, and to everything that creeps on the earth, everything that has the breath of life, I have given every green plant for food. And it was so. (Gen. 1:26–30)

The mandate to "subdue" and to "have dominion" over the earth is an authority to use the earth to further God's plan. It is not a mandate to use power only at our discretion; human power is arbitrary. It is therefore not the power to use the earth irresponsibly. It is power, right, and responsibility *combined*.

We are called to conserve the earth as well as use it to construct a civilization that will enhance God's plans; these concepts are complementary, not in opposition. This use has one primary purpose: to make us free, responsible agents who bring to completion, with the Creator's help, the harmony of the created order for His glory.

Thus, our Faith inspires us not to wait around for God to bring about the perfection of His plans. It is up to us to step up and do all we can to fulfill His plan. God is not going to provide bread for the poor of Somalia by magic. God uses *us* to do so. He is not going to enter the lab and work with nature's elements to produce the best morally acceptable vaccines and medicines to improve health care. He expects *us* to do so. The giver of rationality and freedom isn't going to usurp humanity's power of invention or (civil) lawmaking for the common good. In other words, God's providence is an endorsement of our own sense of responsibility. The grace to succeed is guaranteed, but we must not separate ourselves from the intent of the Giver.

As I reflect on this, a middle-aged woman who stepped up to the plate comes to mind. She entered into the midst of poverty and cruelty and was able to lead a life of faith tied to charity, becoming an instrument of divine providence. She saw the tragic situation around her and listened to the inner voice of God whispering to her, "Something has to be done." Fueled by the faith that can move mountains and confident in the God who provides, she used all her money to rent an old building with a dirt floor. The next day, she went around the neighborhood and offered to teach the children. Her classroom was the old building. She had no desks, no chairs, and no table. Her chalkboard was the dirt floor. She rubbed it smooth with an old rag and wrote on it with a stick. Her motivation was to make the world a better place, to become a disciple of God's providence, and to imprint in peoples' heart the mark of Jesus.

That was just the beginning. Today, more than eighty fully equipped schools, three hundred modern mobile dispensaries, seventy leprosy clinics, thirty homes for the dying, thirty homes for abandoned children, and close to fifty thousand volunteers worldwide are helping to further her vision. The woman, as you may guess, was Mother Teresa, now known as St. Teresa of Calcutta. What St. Teresa did through her apostolate of charity and service, we can also do on a smaller scale in our own everyday circumstances.

God is not going to force bad leaders to become servants of the people, nor will He come down from heaven to overturn the reign of injustice on earth. This is not to say He *cannot* do these things: We know He has the power to do so, and there have been historical circumstances in which He has intervened to change the course of events. But those are exceptional cases. In all likelihood God is not going to come down again to end hardship and poverty in our communities. He will not magically establish a community of justice, peace, and love for us. He will not become the world's economic savior, paying just wages to workers.

Rather, God wants us to become ambassadors of His providence. He desires that we make the world a better place. It is in doing so that we cooperate with divine providence.

We can become conscious and active disciples of God's providence through our ideas, our prayers, and our works. Using these we can "fully become 'God's fellow workers' and co-workers for his kingdom" (CCC 307).

Disciples of Divine Providence

Our Ideas

We can become coworkers in the reign of divine providence through our ideas. Ideas, it is said, rule the world. Ideas can be expressed through language—spoken, performed, or written. They are the vehicle through which God infuses into us plans potent enough to transform our society.

Unfortunately, due to our weak nature and the limitations of human faculties, great ideas can be corrupted. Evil is a deprivation of the good; evil ideas can have widespread and long-term effects on people's ability to pursue the good. The Lord wants us to be open to ideas that will promote life, freedom, peace, and development—ideas that will make the world a better place in which to live. They are ideas emanating from the inspiration of divine providence that build us up in virtue so that we can glorify God with our lives.

How do we harness these ideas when they come? We may share them with our spiritual director or someone spiritually wise. We may write them down. We may speak them to a needy world. We may nurture them and not hinder them. We may develop them and, like great innovators, construct them into ethically-sound and viable products and services for us and for our neighbors. Remember, God has given each of us great ideas because He knows we are the right person for that specific idea, at that specific time, for that specific purpose. Each of us is just a custodian of the wealth He wants to be shared among many. The life of faith inspires us to use all the gifts, talents, and ideas provided by our provident Father.

Special attention should be paid to ideas expressed in words. Words are powerful. God made the entire universe through the power of His word. Life and death, Scripture says, are in the power of the tongue (Prov. 18:21). We must be gracious with the words we speak. They must be seasoned with salt to edify and encourage (Col. 4:6). Even when we must speak against injustice and evil in our society, God expects us to show the light of love as we pursue the justice He demands from an unjust world.

In translating our ideas into word, let the Ultimate Provider be our inspiration; even if we are not comfortable with communicating, He can provide the words if we ask Him in prayer. The most common way to know whether our idea is in accordance with God's providence is to assess whether it is in conformity with the laws of God in nature — that is, natural law. Respect for life, freedom, property, and justice in society are all built on this law, written on the hearts of man and the reality of the natural world.

Our Prayers

How do we cooperate in divine providence through prayer? The Lord Himself told us: "Ask, and it will be given you" (Matt. 7:7). In the temporal order, there is an intimate connection between providence and prayer.

Prayer is not a force emanating from us, as we tend to think. Neither is it our effort to persuade God through our words, ascetic practices, and worship. True prayer is prompted by the Spirit of God Himself, who intercedes for us with "sighs too deep for words" (Rom. 8:26). And if it is the Spirit who directs true prayer, then our spirit is connected to its source and inspiration, in Whom and to Whom we pray.

When we pray, then, we are placing ourselves in the eternal will of God. Consequently, our prayer can transform the world because, as it is the eternal will of the Father to use us to transform the world, so our prayers are naturally part of that will. Our prayers' participation in the eternal will of God is powerful.

Similarly, prayer is a clear recognition of providence, because the person who prays is making a bold statement of reverence for the divine will. "What have you that you did not receive?" (1 Cor. 4:7). When we pray, it is an admission that we are under divine governance and our hope is not essentially in man but in heaven, from where our salvation comes (Ps. 121:1). Whether our prayer takes the form of adoration or supplication or thanksgiving or reparation, it should unceasingly render to Providence the homage that is His due. As we have said, prayer is a testament to a life of faith.

Prayer is cooperation in the divine plan. When we are on our knees, we are submitting ourselves to God's will and desire, both in time and for all eternity. At prayer, our will is lifted up from the limitations of the flesh and the world to the domain of the divine will. There, all selfishness is melted away; the walls of division are broken; and our soul is completely absorbed into the eternal love and governance of God.

Thus, at prayer we are able to become God's channels of grace to those we love and to those who are different or far from us. At prayer, we cease to be the egoistic *I* and become *we*. At prayer, the *I* and the *Thou* (God) meet for an encounter that transforms both us and the world. It is in this process that we discover the incalculable potency of prayer.

Our Works

For our works and actions to resonate with divine providence, they must be purposeful, with a view toward bringing about the goal to which they have been ordered. Our works are the secondary cause through which the ultimate goal of providence is achieved; God is the primary cause. This can be achieved when, in our hearts, there is the power and will to love—and, in our hands and feet, there is a readiness to practice it. To do everything for love—love of God and love of neighbor—is the purpose of life on earth. Is not love what our Lord told us is the summary of the law? (Mark 12:28–31).

The ultimate gift that God has given His creatures is the gift of His love, made flesh in the Son who came and died for us. God's love imbues and amplifies our works, making them capable of transforming society. God expects us to carry His love into a world of hatred and conflict. Thus, whatever we do, let it be done in love and for love.

If we love, we go beyond the dictates of justice. True love incorporates justice, which brings peace and order to society. True love brings about a society in which we become "our brother's keeper." True love makes us sons and daughters of God, and we readily carry out the responsibilities of being co-creators and co-providers. This love is *agape*.

We end this teaching with the poem "Christ Has No Body," by St. Teresa of Ávila:

> Christ has no body but yours,
> No hands, no feet on earth but yours.
> Yours are the eyes with which he looks
> compassion on this world.
> Yours are the feet with which he walks to do good.
> Yours are the hands, with which he blesses all the world.
> Yours are the hands, yours are the feet,
> Yours are the eyes, you are his body.
> Christ has no body now but yours,

Disciples of Divine Providence

No hands, no feet on earth but yours,
Yours are the eyes with which he looks
compassion on this world.
Christ has no body now on earth but yours.

Chapter 11

Made for His Glory

The discipleship of divine providence causes us to reflect the glory of God in our world. One of the most common phrases I hear believers say is that we are made for the glory of God. True enough. But it wasn't until I started writing this chapter — after many hours of prayer, Bible study, and research — that I realized that the meaning of this truth is not as clear to many as I had assumed.

I reached out to my readers and social media followers to ask them what they think it means to be made for the glory of God. Their answers were as revealing as my experience. Most of them simply said, "It is praising God," which is good, but not sufficient. This chapter will explore a crucial aspect of our reflection on faith — one of the main reasons I was motivated to write this book.

So, what does the glory of God mean? Let us begin with Scripture.

In Exodus, the nomadic people of Israel enjoyed the privilege of God's abiding and often visible presence. He led them through the desert with a pillar of cloud by day, and a pillar of fire by night (Exod. 13:20–22; 14:19–24). The word *Shekinah* became a domestic word for describing God's radiant presence — what we would today call His glory. Later on, Moses received the two tablets that became the vivid expression of God's presence among His people and the most sacred objects of the religious faith of the Jews. An ark was to be built in which the tablets would be reposed, following the specifications God gave, placed on the mercy seat in the Holy of Holies.

When, for instance, the Philistines defeated Israel and captured the Ark of the Covenant, the dominant mood of the people was total despair. See the words of Rachel, who suddenly delivered her baby: "She named the boy Ichabod, saying, 'The glory has departed from Israel!' because the ark of God had been captured" (1 Sam. 4:21). On the other hand, the psalmist's profession, "The Lord of hosts is with us; the God of Jacob is our stronghold" refers to a people who were assured of God's abiding presence among them when the Ark of the Covenant was secure (Ps. 46:11).

God's glory, therefore, seems to be His manifestation or revelation to His people, whether as prefigured in the imagery of the pillars of cloud and fire or in the Ark of the Covenant.

Now let's turn to the New Testament. The key insights are the words of the Savior in John 17 — His prayer to the Father:

> I glorified thee on earth, having accomplished the work which thou gavest me to do; and now, Father, glorify thou me in thy own presence with the glory which I had with thee before the world was made. I have manifested thy name to the men whom thou gavest me out of the world; thine they were, and thou gavest them to me, and they have kept thy word. (John 17:4–6)

Jesus brought God glory by finishing the work the Father gave him to do — the work of salvation, which is embodied by belief in the fullness of divine revelation. The glory of God is the very identity of God, and Jesus in the fullness of revelation because He has revealed to humanity the character and identity of God. The Lord Jesus Christ is God's glory revealed. The disciples came to know in time that Jesus was the embodiment and revelation of God. "He who has seen me," the Lord told Philip, "has seen the Father" (John 14:9).

Given all of this, how can we glorify God? Let's examine the Greek roots of the word *glory* for some answers.

The Greek word δοξάζω (*doxazo*) is the verb used for "to glorify" in the Greek Scriptures. The noun form, δόξα (*doxa*), means "glory." The word was not originally a sacred concept; the writers of the New Testament incorporated it into the religious context, giving it a new and deeper meaning. *Doxazo* originally meant "to believe," or "to have an opinion," or "to suspect," as in the impressions one might have of another person. Specifically, it was used in the affirmative sense of a good impression or opinion of someone, and not as much in the negative sense of a bad impression. Thus, *doxazo* is to express a high opinion of someone.

In the New Testament, the Apostles used the word to mean "to value highly," "to exalt," and "to magnify." Although related to the secular Greek usage, it adds to the meaning by extending the appreciation beyond private opinions to outward expressions of admiration.

"To magnify" is an especially important new meaning, since it includes the idea of enlarging or enhancing the object or person. This is like zooming in on an image so that every line, contour, and color is clearer and more visible. Magnifying relates to visibility; exalting or extolling relates to praise. This is where the popular concept of glorifying God through praising Him or worshipping Him with words, hymns, liturgy, or instruments fits in.

Yet another vital meaning of the word *doxazo*, as used in the New Testament, is "to value highly." This expresses the idea of a treasure in the heart, like the parable of the hidden treasure, where one will be ready to give up everything so as to possess what is highly valued.

These three nuances of meaning are contained in the word and will help us in our understanding of what it means to be made for the glory of God. The three senses also relate to the three great acts of responsible human behavior — words, thoughts, and actions. We can glorify God by exalting Him, magnifying Him, and valuing Him as our supreme treasure.

Exalting God

We exalt God with praise, with acknowledgment of His supreme majesty, with acts of gratitude, and with prayer. Praising and worshipping God avail much because, as Scripture says, the Lord is "enthroned on the praises of Israel" — that is, His people (Ps. 22:3). The best way to praise God is to offer Him the Son's sacrifice of praise, which He offered to the Father for us all on the Cross of Calvary. Thus, the Eucharist is the apex of divine praise on earth.

Exalting God also entails talking about God — His words, His actions, and His beauty — as readily as possible. God should be frequently on our lips — more often than any other person in our lives. It is surprising to observe that even among believers, God is usually discussed only as a footnote. People spend much more time talking about sports, movies, academics, and social life than they talk about God. It's unfortunate that even for some experts of

Christian theology, too much time and resources are spent on the study of arcane speculations only distantly related to the source of the study — Christ the Lord. We leave the Christian core in pursuit of something less. It is like a husband who talks to others about everything other than his wife and her life and concerns. More often than not there is a correlation between the people you exalt and the people you talk about. This brings up the uncomfortable question: Do you think and talk more about God or yourself? What does this say about whom you exalt above all others?

Magnifying God

We glorify God by magnifying Him — that is, by making Him more visible to others. In simple terms, to glorify God is to reveal Him to those we encounter and throughout our society. Whatever we do that does not reveal — or, worse, obscures — the holiness and goodness of God frustrates our primary goal. We are primarily made for God's glory, to be His reflection in the world.

Reflections share visual or intellectual characteristics (such as when a writer pens a "reflection" on a topic) with the objects or persons or concepts they mirror. They resemble their origin, even if imperfectly, while pointing back to it. Put simply, reflections make visible what they represent.

This resembles the nature of sacraments: symbols and signs that point to *and effect* a deeper spiritual reality. The Church Herself has this sacramental nature because the "eternal mystery of the divine plan for the salvation of humanity was given its *visible form* as the Church, the new People of God."[32] The Church

[32] John Paul II, General Audience, November 27, 1991, emphasis added.

embodies God's presence among men and at the same time is the sign of the eternal kingdom yet to come. Each member of the Church is a living temple of God, wherein God resides: "Do you not know that your body is a temple of the Holy Spirit?" (1 Cor. 6:19).

The Church is the assembly of God—the new people of God in Christ—and not simply an individual. She is therefore bigger and deeper than each of the individual members. But each member of the Church is integrally connected with the others, for we are one in Christ, members of His Body, the Church. Thus, the Church, as both a community of faith and as a collection of individual members, shows forth to the world the testimony of salvation, which has been won on Calvary. The Church by Her very nature magnifies God through worship, prayer, sacrifice, words, and good works among people.

Similarly, all that exists in the temporal order points to the source of its being—its originator, its Creator.

Scripture and Tradition never cease to teach and celebrate this fundamental truth: "The world was made for the glory of God (*Dei Filius*, can. § 5: DS 3025)." St. Bonaventure explains that God created all things "not to increase his glory, but to show it forth and to communicate it (*In II Sent.* I, 2, 2, 1)," for God has no other reason for creating than His love and goodness: "Creatures came into existence when the key of love opened his hand (St. Thomas Aquinas, *Sent.* II, Prol.)" (CCC 293).

Two distinctions must be made here between rational created beings (i.e., humans and angels) and other creatures in the manner in which God is magnified. Although the world in all its beauty points to its Creator and thereby magnifies Him, and although the very existence of living plants and animals are a testimony of the eternal wisdom of the Creator, these created things do so without will or choice. Humans and humans alone, in the temporal order, are called to magnify the Lord with their will and choices. This happens, it turns out, in the very being of humanity—when the person is fully alive in love and faith and hope. As St. Irenaeus saint puts it, "The glory of God is man fully alive."

The beautiful baroque architectural masterpiece of the Archbasilica of St. John Lateran in Rome reflects the intellect and spreads the name of Alessandro Galilei, the great eighteenth-century architect who designed it. So does Michelangelo's *Last Judgment* in the Sistine Chapel, his imposing statue of *Moses* inside the Church of San Pietro in Vincoli, and his masterpiece *Pietà* at St. Peter's Basilica. And the baldacchino of St. Peter's Basilica, a magnificent bronze canopy over the shrine of the Apostle Peter below the dome, reflects the mind and fame of Bernini. And in their own way the ancient pyramids of Egypt, the great stones of Ethiopia, and the artistry of the Benin sculptures reflect their makers. Each of these masterpieces in different ways gives us insight into the cultures from which they emerged, the genius of those generations, and the creative personalities who conceived of them. In the same way, God's creation reflects and magnifies His nature.

There's no better place in the New Testament to find a testimony to the glory of God than at the church in Antioch of Pisidia, when, through the witness of the early Church, the pagan world came to confess "these are *Christians*" because they follow the footsteps of Christ, their founder (see Acts 11:26). The lives of the early Christians made Jesus so visible that the Pisidians could see Jesus in the lives of the disciples—in their preaching, in their community life, in their prayers, and in their performance of miracles.

The life of the creature has meaning in reference to its Creator. The creature simply cannot live its life to the fullest without revealing its Maker. Thus, our life is most fully lived when it more fully reveals Jesus Christ.

Valuing God as Our Highest Treasure

We glorify God by worshipping Him as our highest, priceless treasure. Nothing—nothing!—can compare to Him. Worship reminds us of our total commitment and loyalty to God, who does not share His glory with anyone else. If we value God as the highest treasure, He sets the standard for our appreciation of other lower values. We can then acknowledge His lordship (Matt. 6:9–13), submit to His Son (Phil. 2:9–11), participate in His work (Hag. 1:7–8), endure anything and suffer for His sake (1 Pet. 4:12–16), and be ready to offer our lives in martyrdom (John 21:18–19; Ps. 116:15).

Martyrdom (from the same Greek root word for "witnessing") is the clearest evidence of one who treasures God above all else. If we really take God as our highest treasure, then nothing will ever take His place in our lives. In fact, we will be willing and ready to sacrifice everything, including our lives, for God's cause.

The Benefits of Glorifying God

God has made us for Himself, and the glory of humanity is a society that glorifies God. When we glorify God, we become the best we can be and achieve harmony in a world ruptured by sin and wickedness. Otherwise, God's name is made an object of scorn among people and the revolt against Him makes humanity the most vulnerable of all creatures. The result is conflict between a person and his neighbor, and between mankind and the natural world.

The story does not end this way for the person who has undertaken the life journey of faith. Instead, we experience joy and fulfillment as God is praised, worshipped, and magnified through us. Faith, by glorifying God, makes us the very best we can be.

The life of faith and the journey of faith are one and the same: humanity living the way God has made us to be, experiencing the joy of salvation in anticipation of blessed eternity. This is glory at its best.

About the Author

Fr. Maurice Emelu

Fr. Maurice Emelu is a Nigerian priest of the Catholic Diocese of Orlu and the founder of Gratia Vobis Ministries, a global ministry for the New Evangelization and for works of charity. The author of three books, Fr. Maurice is also a theologian, providing robust crosscultural Catholic evangelization programs through new media and public speaking. In addition, he teaches leadership and managerial skills in the nonprofit administration program at John Carroll University near Cleveland, Ohio. He has appeared on television on EWTN and KNXT (Fresno, California), and on Catholic radio. Most importantly, he is an African priest passionately in love with Christ and His Church.